The
Politics
of the
Barrios
of
Venezuela

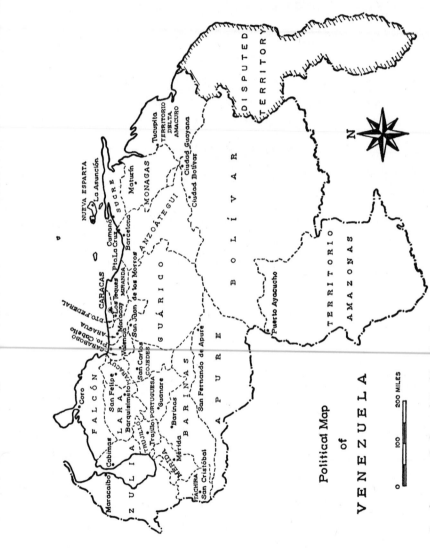

Political Map
of
VENEZUELA

0   100   200 MILES

Based on map © General Drafting Co., Inc.

THE
POLITICS
OF THE
BARRIOS
OF
VENEZUELA

Talton F. Ray

University of California Press
Berkeley and Los Angeles
1969

University of California Press
Berkeley and Los Angeles, California
University of California Press, Ltd.
London, England
Copyright © 1969, by
The Regents of the University of California
Library of Congress Catalog Card Number: 69-12844
Designed by Steve Reoutt
Printed in the United States of America

Preface

The *barrios* are the squatter settlements that are clustered in and around every city in Venezuela. In them live most of the hundreds of thousands of poor peasants who have migrated to the cities from rural areas during the last twenty-five years. Part I of this study provides background information regarding this migration and examines briefly the physical, economic, and social conditions of the barrios. Part II analyzes the political behavior and attitudes of the barrio dwellers and describes how these have been affected by the urban environment, in particular by the process of modernization, by the municipal and state governments, and by the political parties. Part III assesses the role that the barrios have played in national politics and, drawing on evidence presented in Part II, examines certain problems related to their current political status.

The shantytowns are not peculiar to Venezuela. They are a phenomenon common in varying degrees to every country in Latin America (as well as to most of those in Africa, the Middle East, and Asia) [1] although their names may be different. In Mexico these settlements are called *colonias proletarias*, in Chile *poblaciones callampas*, in Argentina *villas miseria*, in Brazil *favelas*. Different also are many of the influences that come to bear on their inhabitants. The stages and rates of industrial development, for instance, vary a great deal from country to country, as do the types of political systems, the character and number of the political parties, and so forth. Fundamentally, however, all the inhabitants are in the same predicament. Having moved from their rural homes with hopes of acquiring the benefits of urban life, they have been stopped far short of their goal. They live on the margins of their respective cities—economically, socially, and politically, as well as physically. It was largely the appreciation of the ubiquity of this problem that made me decide that a thorough analysis of the barrio situation in Venezuela would be valuable.

This study is an outgrowth of the two and one-half years (1961–1964) I worked with a private, nonprofit, urban community development organization called ACCION en Venezuela. Initially as a community worker, and later as Director of Field Operations responsible for the selection of project sites and the supervision of ACCION workers, I became personally and, in many cases, intimately familiar with the community life of some 130 barrios in sixteen major towns and cities. The idea of embarking on the study occurred to me while I was still in Venezuela, but the writing was done after my departure. There were four main primary sources for the material on which it is based: (1) my observations of the daily political behavior of the barrio residents; (2) innumerable conversations with men and women of the barrios as well as with officials, social workers, and other outsiders who were in contact with barrio residents; (3) the project reports of the ACCION workers; and (4) individual censuses taken by barrio leaders in conjunction with ACCION workers.

Since the material derived from these sources was a product of my community development work, and not of a carefully planned research project, it lacked regularity and formality. However, by virtue of its multiplicity it did lend itself well to rigorous analysis. Because it was gathered from a large number of different locations, each constituting a variation of the same general phenomenon under study, I was continually able to test the validity of hypotheses based on observations in one or two communities in a great variety of other communities. Thus, through a process of repeated contrast and comparison of findings in one barrio with those in another, and in one city after another, I was able to arrive finally at what appeared to be an accurate assessment of the people's political attitudes and behavior.

Besides the information derived from my field experience, I relied also on published and mimeographed studies and surveys concerning barrio conditions. However, with a few exceptions they dealt almost entirely either with problems relating to housing, public facilities, and social conditions, or with migration and urbanization trends. Therefore, while they proved quite useful for my discussions of these particular subjects, they provided very little information on the attitudes and behavior of the people themselves. The most notable exception was the survey conducted jointly in 1963 by the Centro de Estudios del Desarrollo (CENDES), Universidad Central de Venezuela, and the Center for International Studies (CIS), Massachusetts Institute of Technology, as part of their research project designed to analyze and synthesize the Venezuelan polity. The survey focused on twenty-four occupational and social groups, one of which was the barrio dwellers. The barrio sample consisted of 258 interviews with persons 18 years or older in four barrios, two in Caracas and two more in Maracaibo. Although the results of this sample had not yet been published when I was preparing this study, Professor José Silva Michelena, a director of the project, kindly permitted me to see them.[2] A number of the survey questions were related to topics with which my study is concerned and where the survey and its findings are cited I refer to it as the "CENDES-CIS survey."

I have many persons to thank for their help in making this project a realizable goal. Unfortunately, the people who have made the largest contribution cannot be named individually. These are the hundreds of barrio residents with whom I have worked and talked during my time in Venezuela. Each, unknowingly, has left his imprint on the following pages. Also among those who must go nameless are the many Venezuelans who lived outside the barrios—the local and state officials, businessmen, social workers, and priests—and who added a great deal to both my understanding and appreciation of their country and its politics.

A number of unpublished papers and studies concerning shantytown settlements in Latin America and other developing areas were made available by John C. Turner and Charles Abrams who generously opened their collections to me. At various stages the manuscript has been read by persons who are closely familiar with the socio-political life of urban Latin America and their comments and criticisms have been of invaluable assistance. For this I would particularly like to thank Anthony Leeds, Richard R. Fagen, Douglas Chalmers, José A. Silva Michelena, and Daniel Goldrich. For keeping me abreast of new events and changing conditions in the barrios I am grateful to Michael Bamberger, Luis Finol, Arthur Spiegel, Alfredo Landaeta, Winifred Blatchford, Oswaldo Fernández, Rigoberto González, José Mas, and Edith Humphreys de Mas. For a thorough and no doubt very tiring editing job, I want to express my appreciation to Lynda S. Bridge and Nancy Griffin.

The opportunity to work in Venezuela and to become so closely involved in the life of the barrios was made possible by ACCION en Venezuela, and for this I am especially thankful to the organization's founder and former director, Joseph H. Blatchford. Finally, I owe my greatest debt to my wife, Lilli Doberstein Ray. Her exacting criticism, coupled with constant encouragement helped immensely in every phase of the work.

TFR

Contents

Illustrations follow page 78

Important Dates
in Venezuelan
Contemporary Political History

1908—Beginning of Juan Vincente Gómez' rule.

1918—Birth of petroleum industry, with discovery of oil near Maracaibo.

1931—Venezuelan Communist party (PCV) organized.

1935—Death of Gómez; General Eleázar López Contreras assumes presidency.

1941—General Isaías Medina Angarita succeeds López Contreras. Acción Democrática party (AD) formed.

1945—Medina regime overthrown; AD-dominated government installed, headed by Rómulo Betancourt. Unión Republicana Democrática party (URD) founded.

1946—Social Christian party (COPEI) founded.

1947—Venezuela's first free national election; AD candidate Rómulo Gallegos elected President.

1948—Gallegos removed by coup; military junta led by Lt. Col. Carlos Delgado Chalbaud established.

1950—Delgado Chalbaud assassinated. Junta member Colonel Marcos Pérez Jiménez consolidates power.

1952—Pérez Jiménez annuls national elections won by URD with support of outlawed AD party. Pérez Jiménez assumes full dictatorial powers.

1958—Revolution overthrows Pérez Jiménez regime January 23. Provisional Government is headed by Rear Admiral Wolfgang Larrazábal. Betancourt, AD candidate, wins national election in December.

1959—President Betancourt inaugurated in February. AD-COPEI-URD coalition formed.

1960—AD youth wing splits off, forming Movimiento de Izquierda Revolucionaria (MIR). PCV and MIR initiate violent subversive activities. URD abandons coalition.

1962—Another AD faction, led by Raúl Rámos Giménez, splits off and forms Acción Democrática en Oposición (AD-OP). Garrisons rebel at Carúpano and Puerto Cabello. PCV and MIR members launch urban and rural guerrilla warfare in name of Fuerzas Armadas de Liberación Nacional (FALN).

1963—AD candidate, Raúl Leoni, wins December election. Frente Nacional Democrática (FND) and Fuerza Democrática Popular (FDP) parties formed. PCV and MIR outlawed.

1964—President Leoni inaugurated. AD-URD-FND coalition formed.

1966—MIR dissolves. FND abandons coalition. PCV adopts nonviolent tactics.

1967—Faction led by Luis Beltrán Prieto Figueroa abandons AD and later forms party, Movimiento Electoral del Pueblo.

1968—National elections scheduled for December.

Glossary

abasto—grocery store, somewhat larger than a bodega

ACCIÓN en Venezuela—a private, nonprofit, urban community-development organization

Acción Venezolana Independiente—a political organization representing the interests of the Venezuelan business community

adeco—member of the AD party (Acción Democrática)

"asesino comunista"—"communist murderer"

Asociación Pro-Venezuela—a political organization representing the interests of the Venezuelan middle-class

barriada—urban squatter settlement in Peru

barrio—urban squatter settlement in Venezuela (literally, "neighborhood")

bienhechuria—land improvement which serves to establish a squatter's rights to a plot of land

bodega—small grocery store

cacique—local political strong man

campesino—poor peasant

campo—countryside

caserio—small rural settlement

caudillo—nineteenth-century Latin American leader who used the personal loyalty of his followers to consolidate military and political power, either regionally or nationally

cayapa—communal work day, mobilized in both barrios and campesino settlements to make some basic community improvement, for installing a water system or repairing a street, for example

colonia proletaria—urban squatter settlement in Mexico (literally, "proletarian colony")

comité de barrio—the smallest unit of the AD party, at the barrio level

compañero—comrade, used by fellow members of the AD party

Confederación de Trabajadores de Venezuela—the dominant national labor organization, composed of numerous labor federations of the petroleum workers, construction workers, etc.

conuquero—campesino, specifically, one who subsists on the produce of a small plot of land to which he does not hold title

coreano—person from the city of Coro (Falcón State) or its environs

coronel—colonel, used in the honorary sense in rural Brazil in recognition of political influence

Dividendo de la Comunidad—a national fund for social programs, supported by contributions from private companies

"el que manda"—"the one who runs the show"

engañado—deceived

evangélico—Protestant convert

favela (Portuguese)—urban squatter settlement in Brazil

Federación de Cámaras de Comercio y Producción—National Association of Chambers of Commerce

Fé y Alegría—private, Roman Catholic church organization (meaning "Faith and Joy") which provides free education to barrio children

hacendado—owner of a hacienda

hacienda—country estate or farm

hato—ranch, especially one which raises cattle

Instituto Venezolano de Acción Comunitaria (IVAC)—a private, nonprofit community-development organization

jefatura de la parróquia—precinct headquarters, *parróquia* being a political subdivision, of which there are ten in Caracas *junta*—an elected community council, usually of seven members

Junta Pro-Mejoras—Pro-Betterment Junta, a common name for barrio juntas

lyceo—high school

manifestación—mass political demonstration

mirista—member of the MIR party (Movimiento de Izquierda Revolucionaria)

Movimiento Pro-Desarrollo de la Comunidad—the junta federation in Caracas

paralelismo—technique whereby local governments undermine the opposition by establishing parallel organizations which compete with those of the opposition

patrón—man who demands the respect of his social inferiors and who assumes paternal responsibilities for them

población callampa—urban squatter settlement in Chile (literally, "mushroom settlement")

político—politician, especially one considered shrewd and opportunistic

por puesto—taxi which operates like a bus along a specified route and charges each passenger a fare

por su cuenta—on his own account

prefecto—district or municipal police chief

prefectura—the office of the prefecto

quebrada—a dry creek bed, most of which in Caracas are crowded with ranchos

rancho—the shack home of a barrio dweller

simpatizante—person who sympathizes and votes with the AD party, but is not a member

superbloque—large, multi-story apartment houses built for barrio dwellers by the Pérez Jiménez government

tarjeta grande—"big" ballot, cast at the national election for a presidential candidate

tarjeta pequeña—"small" ballot, cast at the national election for a political party

urdista—member of the URD party (Unión Republicana Democrática) *ventajismo*—the use of government authority for the advancement of the party in power

villa miseria—urban squatter settlement in Argentina (literally, "village of misery")

vocal—member of a barrio junta who holds no special title, such as president or secretary

I

The
Setting

1

Introduction

Venezuela is passing through a critical phase of its history. At
the same time that it is undergoing the strenuous task of
developing into a modern, industrial nation, it is also trying
to forge an effective and stable democracy out of political
traditions that for centuries have been authoritarian.[1] One of
the elements in today's society that will play an important
role in determining the success or failure of Venezuela's attempt at political reform is the people of the barrios—the
dwellers of the vast squatter settlements that blanket the
fringes of every town and city.

Most people see the barrios only from the outside, as they
drive past on the main roads or gaze out from the windows of
their homes and offices. The shacks can be seen clinging to
the hillsides overlooking Caracas and San Cristóbal, huddling
along the water's edge near Porlamar and Ciudad Guayana,
and extending for miles on the flat land surrounding the
central districts of Maracaibo, Barquisimeto, and Ciudad
Bolívar.

The motley of colors reveals the materials with which the
shacks are made: wooden slabs, cardboard, aluminum sheet-
ing, and flattened tin cans. Some are built of mud and sticks,
a few of concrete or cinder blocks.

In many cities, particularly those where land is scarce and
hilly, there is no apparent pattern to the way the shacks are
arranged. They are crowded up against one another, leaving
no room for anything but miniature footpaths which one sees

as they appear and disappear winding through the maze. Few people are in sight; one wonders where they are, how many there are, and what they are doing. On a clear day, when the sun dances off the aluminum rooftops, one senses an air of sociability and even gaiety about these clusters of tiny homes. In the winter, when the skies darken with rain clouds, an aura of utter dreariness prevails.

In other cities, where the land is level and relatively abundant, the shacks are more comfortably distributed, with enough space between them for dirt streets. Shrubs and an occasional tree are scattered about and offer some relief to the monotonous scene. The shacks here have a more permanent appearance, but one still hesitates to call them "houses." Pigs and dogs scurry down a street, and one glimpses naked brown children.

Travelling by on the main roads at night, one can easily remain oblivious of the barrios' existence. The flickering of light from an open doorway or an occasional street lamp gives some sign of life, but there is no hint that thousands of people sleep there in the darkness.

The history of the formation of the barrios falls into three fairly well defined stages which correspond to the various waves of migration of *campesinos* (poor peasants) into the urban areas. The migration itself has tended to respond sensitively to both rapid economic development and transferals of political power.

Prior to 1945, and especially after the early 1920's when the exploitation of oil began to transform Venezuela's economy, there had been a perceptible and significant movement from the countryside to the cities, but it was neither rapid nor concentrated enough to give rise to the extensive settlements known today as barrios. The first major wave of migration was triggered by a political event, the coup of October 1945 that brought down the regime of General Isaías Medina Angarita and established in its stead the first administration in Venezuela's history that actively sought the support of the populace.* For the landless campesino, who until then had been totally ignored by the successive governments, this marked the dawn of a new era, and many took advantage of the aura of freedom that suddenly prevailed to gather their belongings and travel into the cities where they expected the new government would be anxious to respond to their desire for jobs, free land, and education. During this early period, most roads led either to Caracas or to the oil towns in the Oriente and around Lake Maracaibo. Unable to afford the luxury of moving into established residential areas, the new arrivals organized themselves in groups and settled clandestinely on vacant land that was either publicly or privately owned. The *ranchos* (as the shacks are called in Venezuela) that the migrants built represented their claims to the seized property. This process of illegal settlement is commonly called an "invasion," and it is the method by which almost all barrios have been formed. Since it is essentially a political act, it will be discussed at some length in Part II, Chapter 3.

The second wave of migration ran approximately from 1950 through 1957. Although this period roughly corresponds to the years that President Marcos Pérez Jiménez exercised complete control over national politics, the stimulating effects of rapid economic development were more than enough to offset the restrictions imposed by the dictator, and the rate of urbanization further accelerated. As a consequence of a great surge in oil production (it doubled from 1950 to 1957)[2] and the expansionist economic policies adopted by Pérez Jiménez,[3] the economy began to grow with extraordinary speed. The Gross National Product increased by 95 per cent,[4] giving Venezuela the highest rate of growth in Latin America. As more and more money was poured into

* In a survey taken in late 1958, 3,035 families in Caracas (all of whom had lived at one time in some of the city's oldest barrios and many of whom still lived in barrios) were asked how long they had resided in the capital. The average length of stay was thirteen years, a fact that testifies to the remarkably close correlation between the first major wave of migration and the political events of 1945. (J. Sahagun Torres, "Encuesta Sanitaria del Sector Oeste de la Urbanización 23 de enero," cited in [23].) Bracketed numbers in footnotes refer to publications listed in the Bibliography.

the economy and the demand for a wide variety of goods and services swelled, the cities became bustling centers of activity. The construction industry boomed, and there was a rapid expansion of commercial enterprise and government administration.* When word of these developments reached the countryside, where living conditions had remained largely unchanged, it stirred latent aspirations of young and old alike, and the pace of migration picked up quickly.

The third and latest wave of migration began in January 1958 with the overthrow of the Pérez Jiménez regime, and demonstrated once again the close connection between political change and urbanization. When the leaders of the Revolution turned the government over to a popularly oriented military-civilian junta, the movement of campesinos toward the cities, which thus far had been substantial by any standards, suddenly grew to tremendous proportions. So concentrated was the trend that today more barrios trace their origin back to those first twenty-four months following the Revolution than to any other period. Migration has subsequently decreased, but there is still a continual and heavy flow of campesinos to the urban areas.

When measured against the experience of other Latin American countries, migration in Venezuela has been extraordinary. Two aspects are especially noteworthy—its pervasiveness and its magnitude in proportion to the total population. Whereas in many other countries migration has tended to flow toward one or two of the major population centers, it has been a nationwide phenomenon in Venezuela.[5] In 1950 there were only six cities that had more than 50,000 inhabitants, but by 1961 this figure had increased to

---

* In Venezuela as a whole, urbanization during this period was only slightly stimulated by industrialization, which in the 1950's was still not well enough advanced in the urban areas to constitute a real attraction to rural residents. A minor exception was Valencia; a major one was Ciudad Guayana, where the iron-mining industry attracted many families from nearby states. The importance of the non-industrial sector in promoting urbanization is noted by Emrys Jones [24], p. 421. For a lengthy discussion of the close correlation between the growth of tertiary activities and urbanization in Latin America in general, see Denis Lambert [122]. See also Waldemiro Bazzanella, [98].

sixteen. The number of cities over 20,000 doubled during the same period, from twenty to forty.[6] As Emrys Jones has pointed out, there were in 1940 only four Venezuelan states where the majority of the population were urban dwellers, and only one more had been added by 1950. But in 1961 the number had increased to thirteen.[7]

Although no statistics specify the total number of migrants who moved from rural to urban areas, the following figures are good indicators. During the period 1950-1965, when the nation's population grew from 5 million to 8.7 million,[8] the proportion of urban dwellers increased from 48 per cent to 66 per cent.* Or, more vividly, during the same period, the number of town and city residents increased by 3,300,000 (this figure includes approximately 340,000 officially recognized immigrants,** or 138 per cent, whereas the number of country residents increased by only 360,000, or 14 per cent. Using these figures and certain assumptions regarding the rate of natural increase of the migrants and foreign immigrants, it is possible to determine that slightly more than one million persons migrated into urban areas during the sixteen-year period ending in 1965.[9]

Not all the migrants, of course, were poor campesinos who settled in the barrios. As the CENDES-CIS survey revealed, a significant number were from relatively prosperous rural families,[10] and they undoubtedly moved into the established sections of the cities. Nevertheless, one can be sure that the great majority did in fact become rancho dwellers, since the barrios today house between one-third and three-quarters of the populations of their respective cities. Official estimates indicate the following percentages for some of the major

---

* "Urban" is defined by Venezuelan statisticians as a town with over 2,500 inhabitants. If 5,000 were to be the lower limit, the number of urban residents would be about five per cent less. See [89], Cuadros 139 and 134.

** The number of officially recognized immigrants represents the net gain of arrivals over departures of foreigners, 1950–1965, virtually all of whom, we can assume, settled in urban areas. For the years 1950–1959, see [48], cited in [64], p. 473, Table S.10; for 1960–1965, see [89], Cuadros 414–417. The figures cited do not include, of course, illegal entrants, most of whom were Colombians who settled in the western Venezuelan states of Táchira and Zulia.

cities: Caracas, 35 per cent; Maracaibo, 50 per cent; Maracay, 70 per cent; Puerto La Cruz, 44 per cent; Cumaná, 63 per cent.[11]

The new settlers have one overriding preoccupation—they want to share as fully as possible in the benefits that urban life has to offer: jobs, free land, education, running water, fancy clothes, cheap diversions, and so forth. While a few of them have been fairly successful in realizing this aspiration, the great majority live in conditions that are only a notch or two better than those in the rural areas. The longer they are denied these urban benefits, the more anxious they become, and what is initially mild disappointment can develop with time into bitter frustration.

In the Venezuelan political system, under which every adult citizen has the right to vote, this frustration is expressed at the elections. It is expressed as well by all of the major political parties, each of which professes eagerness to champion the barrio cause. Most important, the party leaders can convert it into political action. In the light of these considerations, it is not difficult to see that the barrios can have a powerful impact on the future of Venezuelan politics. One of the aims of our study is to assess what sort of impact this is likely to be.

For the political analyst, the people of the barrios present certain unique problems. These problems are suggested immediately just by the difficulty of finding suitable nomenclature that accurately describes them. "Working class" and "proletariat" for obvious reasons are not satisfactory. Even the term "urban lower class" attributes a characteristic to barrio residents that most cannot rightfully claim. Recently scholars and writers have searched for more appropriate names and have come up with such terms as "marginal elements," and "urban peasants," but likewise each of these has certain limitations.

In addition to this minor difficulty, it is clear that the criteria traditionally used for analyzing the politics of the lower sectors of urban society in industrialized countries cannot be appropriately applied to the barrio dwellers. The great majority are not members of trade unions, and, therefore, attempts to correlate the political significance of this sector with the growth and activities of organized labor during the last two decades are bound to yield inaccurate conclusions. Neither are they participants in or followers of a socialist movement, or of a single socialist party, whose leaders, organization, platform, and electoral support could be analyzed to give an insight into barrio politics. Instead, their allegiance is divided among a number of different parties, all of which advocate highly progressive programs to advance the welfare of this sector.

While the unions and parties are not suitable objects of study for our purposes, there is another "institution" that can offer a very revealing picture of the people's politics—the individual barrio. The vast conglomerates of ranchos massed around the cities are divided into numerous separate communities. In 1966, Caracas, for instance, had some 254 individual barrios, Maracaibo 108, and Valencia 74. Each is limited by certain informal but usually definable boundaries, and each has its own name.

The number of inhabitants of most barrios ranges between 1,500 and 2,500. The most populous single barrio is *"Isaias Medina Angarita"* on the western hills of Caracas, with an estimated 18,000 persons. Few barrios have less than 150 inhabitants. The density of population varies considerably. Ranchos are most tightly packed together in the gullies and on the hillsides of Caracas and San Cristóbal. On the other extreme, *"Sierra Maestra"* in Maracaibo, for example, is spread out over several square miles and has room for wide, straight streets and spacious lots. Official surveys in different cities indicate that the average number of persons living in one home is six.

Our attention will be focused on these communities, for they afford the most revealing, as well as most accurate, view of the political behavior of their inhabitants. Each barrio is a small political arena with leaders and followers, and a constant interplay between groups of different allegiances. Every barrio has had at one time a semblance of a representative body, and usually an election has been held. The political parties all compete actively. There are many opportunities for the residents to take cooperative action, especially in connection with community improvement. One can assess why they very seldom take advantage of these, and, when they do, what motivates them. From within the barrio one can get the best view of what its inhabitants expect from the government, and what they actually receive from it. In short, each barrio offers ample evidence of the aspirations, antagonisms, disillusionments, and conflicts that are at the base of the people's political life.

2

General Barrio Conditions

Physical Conditions

When one compares the living conditions of families in different barrios, in different cities, it is obvious that some of them have been much more fortunate than others in the opportunities they have had to take advantage of the amenities of urban life. Their private and community facilities are in widely varying stages of development. The two factors which are most responsible for the variation are the terrain on which a particular barrio is built and the age of the barrio.

The more steep the terrain, the more difficult it is for the settlers and the government to cope with the basic tasks of house construction, building and maintenance of streets, and installation of water and electric systems. Barrios constructed on hilly terrain also face grave dangers from the heavy rains which can wipe dozens of ranchos off a hillside in a few hours. Therefore, if we consider only the natural difficulties of barrio living, the families of Caracas and San Cristóbal are probably worse off than those in any other city.[1]

The age of a barrio contributes substantially to the degree of comfort enjoyed by its inhabitants. Unlike the typical slum quarters of industrialized cities in northern countries, in which old buildings with once-satisfactory facilities have deteriorated over the years, the conditions in most barrios improve with age. In the first stage of development, a barrio consists only of shacks; there are no roads and no water. As time passes, however, such facilities are installed, and houses, instead of degenerating further, assume a more stable appearance as their owners invest in improvements. Each new effort adds something that was lacking before. Understanding this feature is essential for understanding barrio culture and for appreciating the difference between living in shantytowns and in traditional slums, where people typically dwell in rented tenements and conditions deteriorate, rather than improve, with time.[2] As we shall see later, it has a significant effect on the social, and therefore political, outlook of the residents.

Aside from these variations owing to terrain and the age of the barrio, living conditions from one barrio to another are similar in many respects. Streets exist in all barrios where terrain permits. Their layout often reflects some effort on the part of the original settlers to organize their community in an orthodox fashion, and in most areas settled since 1958 a regular street pattern is evident. Until approximately 1965 streets were almost invariably of dirt. Since then, as the consequence of active government programs, a fairly high proportion have been paved.

The conglomeration of construction consists mainly of private homes—ranchos and a few block houses. With the partial exception of Caracas, where immigrant families (principally Italian and Portuguese) have been more enterprising, drugstores, barber shops, dry-goods stores, garages, and the like are usually not found in barrios until they are in the last stages of progress. The only commercial establishments that are commonly seen are the bars (*botiquines*) and *bodegas* (or *abastos*) The latter are tiny grocery stores, customarily attached to the homes themselves, which sell such basic commodities as bananas, bread, coffee, yucca, canned goods, kerosene, cigarettes, beer, and sandals.

Most families have access to electricity for private consumption. Except in cases where power lines are illegally tapped, individual meters determine the monthly rates. It is a rare community, however, that has street lighting. A much smaller portion of families have immediate access to running water. That "precious liquid," as barrio mothers like to call it, is customarily brought in by truck. If the service is a private operation, the water is sold for one to two bolivars (22 to 44 cents) per oil drum; if it is provided by the municipal council, the water is distributed free of charge. On hills too steep for trucks, mothers and children carry their water up in tin cans and buckets. Where running water is available, one-spigot fountains are installed at intervals throughout the community; families seldom have pipes extending into their homes.

On level land, about one-third of the ranchos have latrines. In a still small but gradually increasing number of Caracas barrios, elementary sewer systems are in use. Elsewhere, simpler and far less sanitary methods are used.[3] Until quite recently, regular trash disposal was rarely provided. Women customarily found a convenient spot near their homes to dump garbage. However, municipal authorities in some cities are now undertaking to collect trash once or twice a week. Nevertheless, since the collection is made only at a few central points in each community, the service is still far from adequate.

Every barrio aspires to have a school of its own to provide an education for at least the first three grades. It is safe to estimate that two-thirds of them have yet to realize this goal. Public transportation services infrequently extend into the barrios themselves. Usually the people have to walk out of their communities to one of the main roads to catch a bus or *por puesto,* a combination taxi-bus, which carries them to the downtown sections.

When a sample of barrio dwellers was asked by the CENDES-CIS interviewers what they thought was the most important thing to do to better living conditions in the barrios, it was these facilities—particularly water, paved streets, and electricity—about which they were most concerned. By comparison, the condition of their ranchos was of only minor importance to them.

Aspects of Economic Life

For one accustomed to the orthodox expansion of urban centers by the gradual extension of paved streets, water mains, and sewer systems, and the construction of buildings and houses, it is difficult to imagine a community of 3–5,000 persons being annexed to a city almost overnight without any of the city's surveyors, architects, contractors, bankers, and carpenters participating in its development. Such is the case with most barrios, which are brought into existence, autonomously as it were, with little or no help from the outside business world. Much of the material for the ranchos is scavenged; if some must be purchased, the seller is often another barrio resident who makes a small profit on scraps he has managed to collect. Any planning deemed necessary for distributing lots and locating streets is carried out spontaneously by several settlers equipped with a long tape measure. The building of streets themselves requires only machetes and picks, and the work can be handled easily by the new dwellers. In short, a community of 500 separate homes can be constructed within two or three days without the city's commerical interests being any more than visually aware of it.

Like a new barrio, which springs up without any apparent relationship to the economy of the surrounding city, the newly arrived migrant is also totally detached from the urban economy. When the campesino decides to move to the city, he does so of his own accord. Nobody, except perhaps his family, urges him to give up his old home; in fact, government agencies would like to discourage this exodus. Private industries have no recruiting programs that go out into the countryside looking for prospective employees. The migrant almost never secures a job before he actually establishes his new residence. Sometimes he comes alone to scout the possibilities, bringing his family after he finds employment. Usually, however, the appeal of urban life overrides such caution and the campesino, accompanied by his family, arrives in the city without a job or a place to live.

Studies of squatter settlements in other countries of Latin

America have indicated that in most of them there is a high degree of small business activity. In a recent article, which is the best survey to date of published and mimeographed material in this general field, William Mangin writes of "a tremendous proliferation of small enterprises" in such settlements and portrays the shantytowns as bustling centers of trade which house everything from banks and movie theaters to garages, barber shops, and bakeries.[4] Implicit in his description is the idea that many of the residents are highly active petty entrepreneurs. These comments are worthy of special mention because they describe a situation which contrasts sharply with that which is prevalent in Venezuela. While there are, to be sure, numerous bodegas and bars in most communities, there is little else in the way of business establishments. Almost all shopping for items other than a limited variety of groceries must be done in the downtown areas, usually at the central, open-air market. In barrios where small businesses are in operation, as in some of the older, well-established communities of Caracas, the proprietors are often Italian or Portuguese immigrants.

The relative scarcity of small-scale enterprises is curious in view not only of the contrast with other countries but also of the fact that in certain respects the barrios offer an ideal climate for profit-making ventures. A new business would have virtually no local competition. Since shopping in the community would save the women the time and transportation costs of travelling to and from the downtown market, they would probably be willing to pay slightly higher prices. And the enterprising businessman could operate unimpeded by the regulations binding for commercial establishments in the central districts. Yet, despite the apparently favorable conditions, even the long-time barrio residents, men who should be aware of the opportunities, rarely put their imaginations to work for a profit. None of the devious schemes for which these areas would seem so ripe—money-lending, black-marketing, blackmail, monopolistic control of house rentals, and so forth—are practiced with any frequency. Some men do exploit the opportunity to speculate in land, but, as will be seen in the next chapter, the procedure is so standardized that no ingenuity is required.

Studies of the occupational aspirations of Latin American peasants who have recently been introduced to industrialization have almost unanimously found that most migrants desire to be self-employed, to work *por su cuenta*.[5] Unfortunately, no survey of the attitudes of Venezuelan barrio residents on this subject is available. However, it is interesting to note that if they do have the same ambitions as their counterparts in other countries, they are not, at the same time, disinclined to work for large organizations. In fact, a substantial proportion of the adult men, particularly the younger ones, demonstrate a preference for working either for a private industry or for a government agency.* In cities like Ciudad Guayana, Valencia, and Maracay where industry is the major employer, unemployed men often sit idle for months waiting for a job with one of the companies and make no attempt to seek out alternative, more independent means of earning a livelihood. While there is little doubt that this attraction to wage-earning jobs results in part from a lack of financial resources and business experience that would enable men to start out on their own, it can also be attributed to factors of a more positive nature, such as extensive fringe benefits and a regular income, as well as the prestige and respect that are associated with employment in a large firm or agency.

Not surprisingly, the occupational tendencies described here are one of the factors that contribute to the precarious economic position of most barrio families. Wage-earning jobs for the unskilled are in very short supply relative to the current demand, and the situation is not improving since the major sources of employment—government services, public works projects, and private industry—are creating new job opportunities much more slowly than the rate at which the

* While preparing their study of the industrial work force in developing countries, Clark Kerr and his colleagues found to their surprise that ". . . rather than being difficult to recruit, the would-be workers more often were found pounding on the gates waiting to be let inside the new factory system." [170], p. 8.

urban labor force is expanding. As we noted above, only a few of the unsuccessful job-seekers demonstrate the ability or, in some cases, even the desire to find alternative sources of income. Moreover, the form of independent business endeavor which the more enterprising most commonly choose—the bodega—usually provides only the minimal income necessary for a barrio family. A survey of the barrios of eastern Caracas has found that these little stores make on the average about twelve bolivars per day,[6] an income which is roughly equivalent to the daily wage of a manual laborer.

As a consequence of these conditions, unemployment and severe underemployment are high throughout the country. Estimates of the national rate of unemployment vary between about 9 and 14 per cent.* Considering that the middle class sustains virtually none of this joblessness and that the campesinos are employed at least statistically), one can get some idea of the magnitude of the problem in the barrios. A rough estimate of the percentage of unemployed and severely underemployed adult males ranges from about 15 to 20 per cent in some Valencia and Maracay barrios to 70 to 75 per cent in a number of communities in Cabimas where the effects of the slowdown in the once-booming oil industry have been most profoundly felt.**

One of the ironies of the present employment situation in Venezuela is that concurrently with massive unemployment in the cities, there are a substantial number of job vacancies that need to be filled in the expanding industrial sector. The reason, of course, is that many of the available jobs in industry require technical skills that relatively few of the urban labor force have had the opportunity to acquire. In an effort

* There is considerable discrepancy among various statistical sources. For instance, it is stated in the *Plan de la Nación, 1965–1968* ([90], p. 38) that unemployment dropped from 14.4 per cent of the work force in 1962 to 10.5 per cent in 1964. However, the President of the Instituto Nacional de Cooperación Educativa (INCE), in *Publicaciones de la Presidencia, 1961–1964* ([63], p. 104), stated that even if the goals of the 1963–1966 National Plan were fully realized, the unemployment rate would drop only from 14.2 per cent of the work force in 1962 to 13.7 per cent in 1966.

** At one extreme, a census of a Cabimas barrio taken in late 1964 revealed that only three per cent of the 244 families had a member who was fully employed on a permanent basis.

to overcome this structural unemployment and to hasten economic growth, the post-Pérez Jiménez administrations have sponsored training programs, under the auspices of the Instituto Nacional de Cooperación Educativa (INCE), to equip the unskilled for the more demanding jobs. In the early stages these efforts focused on training men who were already employees of private industries. Recently, however, the government has turned its attention toward the unemployed, hoping to relieve the economy and society of the enormous burden created by the annual introduction into the labor market of 100,000 new job hunters, most of whom are unskilled.[7] One of the more effective programs has concentrated on small and medium-sized towns, training men for various types of construction jobs while they work on government housing projects. Since 1964 INCE has also placed heavy emphasis on providing occupational training to young people.[8]

A surprisingly large proportion of the unemployed never earn any money at all on their own, their entire support being provided for by relatives. Others supplement such assistance with a few hours of work on an occasional construction job or by selling fruit, razor blades, ballpoint pens, and the like. Almost all money available to these families is spent on food. The men do, however, have an amazing ability to find enough money to buy a few of their cherished luxuries: a beer or Pepsi Cola, a few cigarettes or a raffle ticket.*

Those whose employment gives them a steady income spend an appreciable amount of their earnings on durable goods. Depending largely upon the ability of a wife to convince her husband that she needs certain items, a barrio family may purchase a refrigerator, a radio, a television, new furniture, a sewing machine, an automobile (to be used as a taxi-bus), or it may invest in improvements on its house. A family usually accumulates just enough money to make the first payment on these purchases or, in the case of house improvement, to buy several hundred concrete or cinder blocks,

* Apparently this special talent for finding some means to support oneself and to make some spending money, even in the face of widespread unemployment, is characteristic of "barrio" dwellers throughout Latin America. See [151] in Hauser [114], pp. 130–131.

a few bags of cement, and a load of sand. Real saving (usually facilitated by a company savings plan) has become a habit with very few families.

The detachment from the urban economy which character- izes the migrants' early days in the city tends to persist even after they become established barrio residents. As a sector of society, the barrio people constitute only a tiny market for goods and services offered by the central districts. Although their numbers have grown enormously in recent years, their impact on the growth of commercial and industrial activity has been relatively weak.

Aspects of Social Life

The social assimilation of barrio dwellers into the cities has been somewhat more successful than their attempts to partic- ipate in the urban economy. This can be attributed in large measure to the quasi-egalitarian attitude that is prevalent among barrio residents, a characteristic that foreign visitors familiar with other Latin American countries consider one of the most unusual attributes of lower-class Venezuelans. This egalitarianism is conspicuous in the people's attitude to- ward their supposed superiors; a barrio dweller does not assume that another man automatically deserves his respect simply because he is an official, a wealthier or more educated person, or a foreigner from one of the "advanced" countries. This outlook has the salutary effect of weakening the diffi- dence that is often characteristic of poor people when con- fronted by members of other sectors of society. The manifes- tations of this attitude are interesting. One sees, for instance the ease with which a group of self-appointed barrio delegates assumes the task of calling on a government official or, occa- sionally, on a company executive when they believe that these men can be of help to their community. They present their request personally and state their case emphatically. They are not awed; in fact, they actually enjoy the role. When uneasiness is apparent, it generally results more from the novelty of the experience than from any notion of social inferiority. Likewise, when an important visitor—a state governor, an upper-class Venezuelan, or even a United States Senator—comes to a barrio, the residents discuss their problems with him freely and try to inform him about aspects of barrio life in which he is interested. Nor are the barrio people unduly impressed by persons who are supposed to possess skills and knowledge which they lack. For example, when an engineer gives them advice on the construction of a school, they will listen to him politely, but if they consider his ideas impractical they will feel no compunction about telling him so and will even offer suggestions for improvements. Similarly, although they are likely to call a North American community development worker with a university degree by the respectful title of "Doctor," they will pay him no more heed than his performance in their community deserves.*

The active role that women play in barrio politics is an important manifestation of the egalitarian outlook and contrasts markedly with the passive role of lower-class women in many other Latin American countries. Women attend community meetings, generally in greater numbers than men; they do not hesitate to voice their opinions; they vote; and many of them are elected to barrio councils. In exceptional cases a woman is even the dominant figure in community affairs, receiving the full respect of her male neighbors. As a general rule, however, their influence is not equal to that of the men, but this can be attributed more to their own lack of assertiveness than to any limitations which their society imposes upon them.

A curious expression of egalitarianism is the women's attitude toward domestic employment. To the surprise of foreign housewives in Caracas, Maracaibo, and Valencia, the average barrio woman is unwilling to work as a maid or cook in a private home, no matter how difficult her economic situation. She would prefer to go without the extra money than to take orders in another woman's household. It is instructive

---

* Lest these comments on egalitarianism be misinterpreted, it is important to mention that barrio dwellers do recognize and follow the direction of leaders. Their allegiance to a certain man, however, is the result of their respect for his personal attributes, and not the result of any innate respect for his rank, education, wealth, or other "acquired" qualities.

to note that the women who most frequently take these positions are from other countries or areas with relatively weak egalitarian values—Spain, Colombia, and the Andean region of Venezuela.

Influenced by the egalitarian outlook, the barrio man feels at ease in the larger society outside his community. He walks through most sections of the city with no sense of discomfort about his clothes or his obvious "barrio" appearance. He does not consider himself the victim of social discrimination. The social assimilation of the barrio residents is, however, by no means complete, and the degree to which it is apparent varies from one city to another. Several factors determine the extent of assimilation.

Where employment is relatively high, men are in daily contact with people from other classes living outside the barrios. They have spending money which enables them to purchase nonessential commodities, and this bolsters their self-respect and their sense of social competence. Were it not for this factor, the barrio families of Valencia [9] and Maracay, for example, would probably feel estranged from the markedly bourgeois social life of their cities.

In small cities certain bonds exist between people in the central districts and those on the fringes that are unknown in the larger ones. For instance, in Ciudad Guayana, members of the Rotary Club (which usually represents a cross section of a city's most well-to-do citizens) frequently talk in their stores and offices with barrio inhabitants; sometimes they greet one another by name. Such familiarity is a remote possibility in Caracas, and, as a consequence, in the capital there is more mutual distrust.

Allegiance to the city's dominant political party can also promote assimilation. Families who feel in touch with the power structure and who know that the officials are "on their side" have a sense of participation in the city's life which those having no confidence in the governing authorities do not experience. This point partly explains the sharp contrast in the degree of assimilation between barrio families in Maracaibo and those in Caracas. In Maracaibo, the dominant party enjoys the almost unrivalled support of barrio residents; because of their feeling of identity with the local power structure, the poorer residents are at home in the downtown area and think nothing of walking into government offices and chatting with the officials. In Caracas, on the other hand, the same party is powerful but has relatively little support on the hillsides; as a result, the barrio families feel politically alienated, and this strengthens their sense of social detachment.

The speed with which shacks are thrown up and new barrios settled might seem to indicate that most of the families are nomadic, constantly moving from one city to another, from one community to another. Generally, however, the moves are quite few and deliberate. When the average migrant campesino leaves his country home, he generally travels no further than the principal town or city in his state or region. For many, particularly the middle-aged and elderly who lack the incentive or financial means to travel on, this is the last move, but some, for reasons of employment, are obliged to take another step. For instance, in 1959 and 1960, when the oil companies had to lay off large numbers of workers, families in cities like Cabimas, Punto Fijo, and Anaco had to abandon their homes in search of jobs elsewhere. The younger and more ambitious, attracted by the reputation of certain dynamic cities, also tend to proceed further. Caracas, the busy, boisterous capital, enjoys such a reputation and consequently it is crowded with families who have come from distant cities like San Cristóbal, Ciudad Bolívar, and Porlamar.* Likewise, the alleged glories of Ciudad Guayana—the boomtown spirit, the high-paying jobs, the nearby diamond fields—entice men to travel across the country from Maracaibo, Valencia, and even Caracas itself.

Even within a city the people do not move around a great deal. In a barrio five years old, for instance, as many as half the families will have lived there, in the same houses, since its

---

* An authoritative study of Venezuelan rural life estimates that very few Caracas barrio dwellers have moved directly from the *campo*, the majority having made several intermediate stops on the way [61], p. 19.

formation, and most of the current leadership will have been actively involved in founding the settlement. Transfer of property is frequent only during the early stage of a new community's life, when speculators sell their lots to people who were not fortunate enough to take advantage of the free land. People value their plots too much to abandon them without some good cause and satisfactory return. New ones are not easy to find, and families are anxious to hold on to what they already have.

Much has been written about the tendency of migrants in the developing areas of the world, in sharp contrast to those in the industrialized countries, to maintain strong ties with the villages from which they have moved. Studies of India,[10] Mexico [11] and sub-Saharan Africa,[12] to mention only a few, tell of nostalgic migrants who frequently visit their old homes and who hope to return permanently when they have earned enough money. Hoselitz, speaking of Asia and Africa, and suggesting that the statment might hold true for Latin America as well, says that the urban peasant "lives in a strange and foreign place as long as he remains in the city." [13] *
If nostalgia among migrants is as common as these studies indicate, then it is clear that Venezuela represents much more the exception than the rule. The great majority of barrio dwellers consider their move permanent, and only a few have an interest in returning to their original homes. Casual discussions about life back in the *campo* are rarely heard except among the oldest of the migrants. "It may be Hell, but I like it!" is a paraphrase of the migrants' most popular quip about Caracas life. The migrants, of course, have not severed all contact with their former homes, but the little they do maintain can usually be attributed to the fact that close relatives (usually parents) have stayed behind, not to their homesickness for the old society.

This characteristic has important political consequences and it is worthwhile therefore to examine its cause briefly.

---

* William McCord expresses a similar view: "Having experienced the desperate emptiness of urban existence, many of them long for a return to the village." [173], p. 40.

The basic difference between the countries mentioned above and Venezuela is not to be found in the cities, as might be thought, but in the nature of life in the countryside. The typical barrio dweller was once what is known as a *conuquero*, a landless campesino who lives off the produce of tiny plots which, thanks to the benevolence of the landowner, he is allowed to cultivate. Although eminently stable by urban standards, his society lacked most of the rich traditions and community social relationships that are characteristic of rural societies in many other countries. Festivals, traditional ceremonies, communal harvests, and church activities were all conspicuously scarce in his life.[14] It is to be expected, then, that the poor peasant who abandons his country home usually feels he has left very little behind.*

The sense of detachment from the countryside which the migrant feels while living in the city is fortified by his lack of close contact with old acquaintances. Relatively few barrios (an exception are those in Cabimas which are inhabited by *coreanos*) ** have large groups of residents who migrated from the same state, much less from the same village or *hato* (estate). The formation of new barrios is such an irregular, unpredictable process that it usually precludes the possibility that groups of friends will find locations in the same community and thus cluster together. Therefore, despite the proximity of barrio homes to each other, relations between neighbors reflect little of the familiarity one might imagine. Families living on the same street, and even next-door neighbors, may never speak to each other. Friendships between mothers are very casual. They meet on the street or at the bodega, but rarely do they visit one another's homes. Men are drawn together not because they live in the same community but be-

* Oscar Lewis distinguished between rural living in Mexico and the United States, saying that "Mexican farmers live in well-organized villages that are more like cities and towns than like the open-country settlement pattern of American farmers." ([124], p. 435). In his respect, Venezuelan rural life resembles the United States' much more than it does Mexico's.

** The *coreanos* come from the environs of Coro, the capital of Falcón State, and have settled in large numbers in the barrios of Cabimas. They are noted for their willingness to cooperate among themselves and to work long and hard hours.

cause they are relatives or members of the same political party, or because they work for the same firm. Only 3.8 per cent of the persons interviewed by the CENDES-CIS survey belonged to a social or sports club. The only occasions when men and women socialize together are baptisms, children's birthday parties, and wakes. Obviously, the social detachment of the Venezuelan migrants contrasts very sharply with the social cohesiveness that one finds among the African migrant tribesmen of Accra and Dar es Salaam, or in the Tepoztlan colony in Mexico City.

Some barrios do reflect a considerable degree of cohesiveness, but there are usually unique explanations for this. For instance, in small, compact, and semi-isolated communities sociability can be high. One also finds a greater degree of familiarity in barrios where there are only one or two entrances, for families frequently meet each other as they walk in and out. Some communities have been closely knit since their formation because most of the residents are the original settlers who had known each other from an earlier barrio. Finally, regardless of the particular characteristics of the barrio, a certain amount of warmth can be generated among the neighbors by their involvement in community projects.

Young people are freer and less selective in their associations than their parents, but their social activities are still scanty. Girls get together and work on their hair or put on fancy clothes and parade through the central market district. When the teen-age boys are not just standing around talking, they get on a bus and wander around the downtown area looking for excitement. Recently some young groups have organized sports clubs, but otherwise they have almost no associations of their own. An interest in political activities partially compensates for this lack of something to do. This is a characteristic that reveals an interesting difference in the behavior of boys and girls. The girls consider community government a social diversion and thus have an inclination to participate in it. They are often members of the small representative bodies, and they take part in barrio commissions that petition the government offices for improvements. The boys, on the other hand, tend to avoid such involvement and prefer to give vent to what political energies they may have by joining in street demonstrations, painting political slogans on city buildings, or carrying out other party functions.

Despite the general absence of sociability within the communities, the barrio people themselves are a fine medium for gossip. Passed along by acquaintances who meet at the market, at work, or in front of the municipal council building, news travels quickly from one area of the city to another. Particularly effective in this respect are the political parties which disseminate news of interest to their members. The extent of communication is perhaps best illustrated by the extraordinary speed with which families from many different communities hear about the settlement of a new barrio and rush to grab up lots for themselves.

Of the formal means of communication, the radio and newspapers are the most effective. A radio is usually the first appliance to find its way into a rancho. Those unable to read the newspapers are told about interesting developments by others who can. Special attention is paid to the one or two pages that carry news about the barrios: a beauty contest, a baseball game, government projects, fights and murders, or petitions to government offices.

Consistent with their campesino background, the educational level of barrio adults is very low. A high percentage have never had any formal schooling, and it is difficult to find a man who has completed as many as seven grades. Though the government is trying to tackle the problem of adult education (using the National Guardsmen as instructors for literacy classes, for instance), the "students'" advanced age and their lack of motivation make the job very difficult. The impressive increase in the literacy rate in the last few years has been primarily because of the accomplishments of the younger generation, whose members (at least in the cities) have had a much greater opportunity to get some schooling than their parents—most of whom appreciate the value of education and have persuaded them to finish the first three grades. Afterwards a substantial number drop out; nevertheless, an increasingly higher proportion of the youth are completing six grades. In the largest cities, especially Caracas, a fair number are carrying on into high school (*lyceo*). There are even a few attending the university.

In general, religion plays a very minor role in the lives of the barrio people. The great majority professes to be Catholic, but only a tiny proportion actively practices its faith. With the exception of the Andean region, priests seldom have close contact with this sector of society. Where they have exerted some influence, as in a few communities in the Tuy Valley, Mérida, Ciudad Guayana, and Caracas, their prestige has resulted more from their dynamic personalities, social progressiveness, and intelligence than from their being representatives of the Church.

Religion, however, does play a vital role in the lives of one portion of the barrio population—the *evangélicos,* or Protestant converts. Each city has little pockets of these dispersed throughout its poorer communities. Their social behavior is conspicuously unique. They congregate on the streets to sing songs and meet in private to discuss their faith. They do not drink, smoke, or even dance. They are notable for their politeness. In communities where such austerity is not common, it is no wonder that the evangélicos should be prominent. Their nominally Catholic neighbors usually consider them aggravatingly proud and condescending, and, although tolerant of their presence, prefer to have little social contact with them. As a consequence, the evangélicos are isolated from most community affairs.

II

Barrio Politics

3

Barrio Formation and
Early Development

The conditions under which barrios have been formed have varied considerably during the three phases of migration. The campesinos who took part in the early phase, between 1945 and 1950, and who moved mainly to Caracas and the towns and cities near the oil fields, met little resistance when they started constructing their rancho communities. The Acción Democrática administration (1945–48) was anxious to maintain and further its support among the poor and therefore tended to be very permissive toward their demands. In addition, established city dwellers were totally unfamiliar with the whole process of rapid urbanization. They had no idea of the enormous changes it would bring to their cities within just one short decade. Consequently they were not overly concerned with restricting the incipient expansion.

However, in the 1950's when the flow of migrants had increased greatly, the situation drastically changed. Pérez Jiménez and his administration were dedicated to maintaining order, and they staunchly defended government and private property. Consequently, the new migrants usually had to seek out worthless bits of land—in the *quebradas* (dry creek beds), under bridges, on abandoned railroad lines, and in marshy areas—and pack themselves in as best they could. Even those who managed to settle in the already established barrios on the hillsides of western Caracas found that they had gained little. The image-conscious dictator thought their ranchos spoiled the new look of the capital, which he was remodelling, so he bulldozed them off their sites and constructed instead gigantic *superbloques* on the barrio hillsides to be rented to the displaced families.*

The Revolution of January 1958 ushered in a new and entirely unprecedented phrase of barrio development. Restrictions on land settlement were immediately lifted, and families poured out of their crowded ranchos to grab up vacant land on the outskirts of the cities as quickly as possible. When campesino families still in the countryside heard about the new opportunities, the flow of migration speeded up tremendously, thus increasing further the demand for new barrios.

Caracas felt the greatest pressure, for it was the focal point of the now famous Plan de Emergencia. Believing that emergency measures were necessary both to cope with the enormous problems of unemployment among the families living in the barrios and superbloques and to meet the high expectations which these people had of the post-Pérez Jiménez regime, the Provisional Government, presided over by Rear Admiral Wolfgang Larrazábal, created vast numbers of new jobs, on public works projects and elsewhere, that guaranteed a daily wage of about thirteen bolivars. In addition, credit was quickly extended to government agencies so that they could provide the barrios with materials for the installation of water lines and the construction of streets and stairways; oftentimes the residents were paid to do the work. Since this assistance was virtually unrestricted, migrants coming in from other cities or from the countryside could take advantage of it as they arrived. In January 1959, almost a year after the Plan de Emergencia had been instituted, an official report esti-

* An official evaluation study of the superbloques done in early 1959 expressed the opinion that they "were built largely out of caprice and personal vanity, impulsively, and with hardly any preparatory studies of an economic, social or urban sort." [10], p. 5. Many of the buildings were not occupied until 1958, when, during the Revolution, they were invaded by barrio dwellers.

mated that each day 100 new ranchos were being erected in Caracas.[1]

In February 1959, the new government, with Rómulo Betancourt as President, took over. Although the Plan de Emergencia was discontinued in August, the government's policy toward the settlers remained lenient and permissive throughout the year. Then the authorities gradually began to tighten the reins, the flurry of excitement subsided, and the pace of barrio formation slowed down appreciably. Yet even today the phenomenon continues. Each city is likely to see one or two new barrio communities settled every year, and the dynamic centers such as Ciudad Guayana, Caracas, and Valencia see even more.

The Formation of a Barrio

The process by which a barrio is formed determines to a high degree the subsequent political life and activities of the residents. Most of the factors which later play an important role in community affairs are introduced at the inception of a barrio, and, therefore, this stage deserves close study.

With a few exceptions discussed later, barrios are created by the illegal possession of public or private land—a mass movement popularly referred to as an "invasion." In some cases, the process of settlement is slow and may take several months to complete. However, in most barrios created since 1958,* the settlement process has been completed within a few days. Since the essential features of development are the same in both cases, we shall concentrate on the more common type.

Although carried out with extraordinary speed which suggests spontaneity, the invasion is a calculated process carefully directed by specific leadership. The outstanding creden-

* The comments in this chapter are based primarily on the writer's observations of barrios that have been formed since the fall of Pérez Jiménez and the establishment of popularly oriented administrations. Not only are these newer barrios more familiar to the writer, but they are far more numerous and of greater contemporary significance. The formation process, moreover, is essentially the same for those barrios settled prior to 1958.

tial of the leader (or leaders) is that he usually has the backing, either tacit or explicit, of one of the political parties that shares governing power in the city. He is not necessarily a member of such a party, but he must be closely affiliated with it. This link is essential because it protects the leader against official reprisal. His connection with a ruling party situates him on the "right" side of the government which, in the final analysis, is the body that decides whether he stays on the land. The government naturally tends to look much more favorably on the actions of one of its supporters than on those of its antagonists. An invasion carried out by independents or under the aegis of an opposing party would represent an open rejection of government authority and, were the action allowed to succeed, it would publicly expose the government's lack of control. To prevent that, officials would send out the police to protect the rights of property owners and remove the settlers from the land. The infrequency with which such force is employed indicates that leaders understand well these political facts of life.

To be sure, there are occasions when government authorities do object to the formation of new barrios and even make some move to drive away the rancho builders. But rather than invalidating the rule, these exceptions actually confirm it. Why? First, because such attempts to thwart invasions are seldom successful. And, second, the reason they are not successful is that the invasion leaders in fact *do* have the support of one of the governing parties, usually that party which controls the municipal council. In a number of cities, including Caracas, the municipal government is in the hands of one party and the state government in the hands of another. If authorities representing the state attempt to squash an invasion led by a member of the municipal party, the latter can usually create enough embarrassing publicity to thwart the effort.

Only by understanding this dispersion of political power at the municipal level among different parties can one understand how the Communists, whose party was numerically very weak, could play such a key role in barrio settlement in

Caracas and other cities in central Venezuela during 1958. Because the party enjoyed considerable influence in various sectors of the Provisional Government, Communists were often allowed to lead invasions. Had they faced officials who were uniformly antagonistic to their party (as they would have, for instance, if the present Acción Democrática leaders had been in power), their efforts would have been quickly frustrated.

Besides being party affiliates, Venezuelan invasion leaders are almost always barrio residents. In some Latin American countries, most notably Peru,[2] it has been observed that middle-class men, usually speculators, frequently plan and execute invasions themselves. The reasons for this difference are not entirely clear, although one obvious advantage of an invasion directed by a barrio dweller himself is that the movement appears to be simply the impulsive demonstration of the demands of the poor for land, dissociated from partisan or speculative interests. This image would not be created were invasions obviously contrived. A more fundamental, but tentative, explanation is that the Venezuelan parties, at least in the urban areas, have succeeded to a relatively high degree in distributing real responsibility and even power downward to their rank-and-file members. The parties' lower echelons do not merely respond to directives from the middle and upper echelons; they are given the freedom to exert a fair amount of control over their own local political activities, as revealed by the initiative of barrio leaders in forming new barrios and creating juntas. The practical importance of this semiautonomy vis-à-vis matters of community concern must not be exaggerated, however, since, as we shall see, the only persons who are able to influence substantially community affairs are those relatively few who enjoy the support of the governing party. The political effectiveness of the members of other parties is severely limited by governmental control.

The leaders' choice of sites further illustrates that the invasions are carefully planned movements. Contrary to what an outside observer may think, leaders do not settle at random on just any vacant piece of land. Before moving onto a site, they learn all they can about its owner, its intended use, and, most important, the attitude of the officials toward its settlement.

During the two-year period following the 1958 Revolution when government officials were anxious to dissociate themselves publicly from policies adopted by Pérez Jiménez and to strengthen their image as true nationalists, many barrios were settled on private land, much of it foreign-owned. This was particularly common in those areas where the holdings of the oil companies were extensive and unoccupied. Later, after the Betancourt administration began to assert its authority and to solicit increased investment from the private sector, both at home and abroad, this practice became much less frequent.

Now when private land is invaded, the leaders are more discriminating and invariably select Venezuelan-owned property. They calculate that the Venezuelan proprietor is usually involved in local politics and understands the subtleties of it. He is, therefore, less likely to press for legal action than a foreigner might be. In one interior city, where a new community was established overnight on the land of a Venezuelan millionaire, invasion leaders explained that they chose the site because its owner had invested heavily in the area. Since his investments were dependent upon political stability, they figured that he would not be quick to stir up trouble. He would know how to arrange for some satisfactory settlement with the officials without calling in the police. Their calculations proved, as usual, to be correct.

In recent years invaded land has usually belonged to the government, and most often to the municipal councils. Not only do the councils own most vacant land in the urban areas, but they also have the closest political connections with the prospective invasion leaders.* The importance of these partisan ties is well illustrated by an example from Ciudad

---

* The close connection between partisan interests and squatter settlements is apparently quite common in other rapidly urbanizing countries as well. See Abrams [157], p. 14, for an opinion on this, and for an example of an invasion in New Delhi.

Guayana. As more families migrated to that city during 1962 and 1963, the demand for space to construct new ranchos increased greatly. Two pieces of vacant land were especially suitable for this: both were government-owned and both had been set aside for future lower-class housing. One of them was under the authority of the Corporación Venezolana de Guayana (CVG), a government agency whose administration was appointed in Caracas and which had no partisan ties with the locally based political powers. The other area belonged to the Banco Obrero, an organization whose partisan connections with the municipal government were intimate; its chief administrator, for instance, was the ex-mayor of the city and one of the most influential members of the party that dominated both city and state politics. Despite the fact that the CVG land was more extensive than that of the Banco Obrero, and despite the growing demand for new land to settle, the barrio families did not touch the CVG property. They did, however, move onto the Banco Obrero land. Their line of reasoning in making this choice was obvious. Since the CVG administrators were not dependent upon popular support and were not committed to back the local ruling party, they would have been able to remove the settlers from their land without fearing the resentment that such an action would create. The officials of the Banco Obrero would be much more inhibited, however, since they were closely linked to the ruling party and would realize that the latter would be adversely affected were they to make any move to squash the invasion.

Sometimes when the barrio leaders are not quite sure of their hold on invaded land, they make the partisan links more conspicuous. For instance, in April 1964, just after the initiation of the second Acción Democrática administration, an enormous tract of land on the outskirts of Maracaibo was settled. Instead of waiting a few weeks to choose a new name for the barrio, as was customary, the leaders immediately posted large signs boldly announcing the formation of *"Barrio Raúl Leoni,"* named, of course, after the newly inaugurated President. They figured that if the whole community openly declared itself in favor of the President, who was the national leader of the party which governed in Maracaibo, the municipal authorities would not dare offend it.

As word of an invasion spreads, families hurry to the area with a few sticks and ropes to stake their claim. Close to 100 per cent of them come from other barrios within the city. Since occupation is so rapid, one can almost categorically discount the possibility of campesinos coming directly from the countryside to settle in a new barrio. By the time they hear about it through relatives, all of the parcels have already been claimed.

Arriving at the site, each family seeks out the leader. He assumes ultimate responsibility for apportioning the land. After selecting a choice spot for himself—on a main street or near the center—and making sure that his lieutenants and fellow party members have their pick, he lets the remainder choose on a first-come-first-served basis.

There are two basic systems used to distribute invaded land, and these partly account for the dissimilar appearance of barrios in various cities. By one system the invasion leaders divide the land into approximately equal parcels (about 10 × 20 yards), with each having at least one side on a street. They are apportioned in an orderly fashion, one to a family. This method is used in cities with relatively flat and extensive land—in Maracaibo, Valencia, Ciudad Bolívar, and Puerto La Cruz, for example. The other system, used in the hilly areas of such cities as Caracas, Puerto Cabello, and Mérida, is less orderly. The leaders who initiate the invasion determine the barrio boundaries, as well as the general course of the streets if terrain permits, and allow the settlers to crowd in as well as they can. A vague but well-heeded rule in this type of settlement says that a family can take space inversely proportionate to the total demand. In many of the Caracas barrios formed on the hills closest to the center of town, the walls of the ranchos touch each other. In the quebradas packed during the Pérez Jiménez days, sometimes as many as four homes are stacked on top of one another. On the other hand, the hill ridges that are inaccessible by automobile and distant from water facilities are sparsely settled. Rancho owners in these areas have often taken enough land to cultivate corn and yucca in their backyards. The observation made by Charles Abrams regarding the ability of urban squatters throughout the world to distribute fairly the land they settle is very appropriate for Venezuela: "Each squatter has exercised a watch over his neighbors' encroachment so that in its chaos the product may nevertheless reflect a multitude of individually imposed controls. . . . Pathways are respected by prospective squatters, and a Ricardian law operates to consume the less and less desirable sites until the most inaccessible or most precarious ones signal the saturation point of settlement." [3]

The system by which parcels are apportioned is of interest not only to urban planners but also to political analysts, for there is a direct relation between it and the political control that is subsequently exercised by the invasion leaders. In the barrios where the flat terrain permits the land to be meticulously subdivided and, consequently, where the allocation of lots is closely supervised, the leaders are able to establish their authority at an early stage. By doing favors for certain persons, by giving them choice parcels, and by settling minor disputes to their advantage, the leader puts them in his debt. This can prove very important later when he needs their support. As we have noted before, in those barrios constructed on hilly terrain, the invasion leaders do not supervise the distribution of lots and thus are in most cases unable to establish their authority at the outset. This is one of the reasons why strong-man, "boss" rule is not generally seen in the hillside barrios of Caracas.

Settlers are given no deeds of ownership for their parcels, and they are asked only to construct some sort of *bienhechuría*, or visible evidence of their intention to build their living quarters on the lot. The settlers usually throw up a small shelter of cardboard or aluminum with a couple of walls and a roof. They then delegate one of the family, generally the mother, to sleep there and secure their place until a more spacious rancho can be built to house the whole family.

In those areas where land speculation is prevalent, one commonly sees a blatant mockery of the bienhechuría—two sturdy poles set into the earth about eight feet apart with a hammock stretched between them.

In 1958, when the invasions were at their peak, the settlers were primarily interested in securing only enough land to build a home for themselves. They sought only to escape the extraordinarily crowded conditions under which the restrictions on barrio settlement had compelled them to live. However, in subsequent years the impulse behind invasions has altered considerably, and speculation is now much more prevalent. As always, the men who led the movements are mostly old-timers who know the ropes well. However, their own desires for more housing space have been largely satisfied, and they claim new parcels of land with the intention of selling them, usually for a handsome profit to families who have recently arrived from the countryside and have taken up residence with their relatives. In an extensive invasion that recently took place in Maracaibo, it can be conservatively estimated that 60 per cent of the 500 original families were speculators, many of them from the adjacent barrio out of which the leader operated. Most admitted this openly and not without a certain amount of pride.

This method of claiming land (that is, by invasion) reveals an oddly ambivalent concept of property on the part of barrio residents. On the one hand, they readily acknowledge that the invaded land still legally belongs to its original owner, and even in a barrio ten years old there are families who will explain that the land is the property of the municipal council or of a particular company. On the other hand, each barrio resident is convinced that his particular parcel is his own private property. Just as he will sell it without compunction, he will defend it as if he had paid dearly for the deed, and this sense of ownership strengthens with the time and effort he puts into improving it. The fact that very few families rent their ranchos is a further indication of the value they place on owning their own lots and living in their own homes. A survey of two Caracas barrios found that between

93 and 96 per cent of the families owned their dwellings,[4] and the overall average for Ciudad Guayana is about 75 per cent. In the barrios of several cities (Maracaibo and Puerto Cabello, for example), renting ranchos is strictly prohibited by the community leaders.

The eagerness with which people seize land for settlement and the extreme informality with which parcels are allocated would seem to indicate that within a community one would have to be continually on guard lest one's own parcel be stolen. Actually the opposite is true. The people have an extraordinary respect for the land and dwellings of other barrio residents, and once a piece of land has a specific "owner," they will not touch it. Evidence of the strength of this respect is seen all over the country. Families reserve choice sites along main roads for years by merely laying the foundation of a house and putting four or five rows of blocks on top. In a barrio in Ciudad Guayana, many residents wanted to construct a kindergarten, but the remnants of a mud rancho—just two dilapidated walls—occupied the only "vacant" lot. Although the owner had apparently left the barrio some ten years before, and nobody had heard of him since, the residents were reluctant to use the land. It finally took the municipal engineer to convince them that it would not be morally wrong to tear down the ruins of the hut.[5]

The people's attitude toward community property is not always so consistent. In some barrios, prospective settlers will not touch lots that have been designated as the sites of communal facilities, such as a school, if they respect the authority of the leaders who have set these lots aside. In one of the largest and most conveniently situated barrios in Caracas, there is an enormous central area that was reserved in 1959 for a school; although at least 50 families could build their ranchos on this piece of land, it has not been settled. But there are also instances where people have poached on community property and no amount of moral suasion has been able to budge them. Again in Caracas, a woman whose house caved in during a heavy rain moved her belongings into the local, one-room schoolhouse, thereby making it impossible for

classes to be conducted. Despite repeated offers of shelter
from her neighbors, she refused to abandon it until the government came to repair her house.

As noted previously, the local governments are usually indirectly involved in the invasions that initiate barrio development. Since most of the land that has been "illegally" settled in recent years belongs to them, their tacit support of
these movements may seem curious; in effect, they sanction
the stealing of their own property. However, if we examine
their motivation, we find that their support of such practices
is actually quite expedient.

Local officials all acknowledge that the barrio population is
increasing. The federal government, through its agrarian reform program, is trying to curb the growth rate by curbing
migration from the countryside, but the movement continues
steadily. Until there are enough housing projects to accommodate the additional families, it is generally believed that
an increase in urban population will produce a corresponding increment in the number of ranchos. There are those
authorities who are determined that this will not happen, but
so far their efforts to enforce restrictions have been ineffec-
tive. For instance, one zealous state governor announced, on
accepting his appointment, that he intended to eradicate all
ranchos in his state and that he was going to begin by not
permitting the formation of another barrio within the capital
city. His police force has been kept busy trying to execute this
policy, but, impeded by the fact that an opposition party
controls the municipal government, it has been almost totally
unsuccessful.

These considerations have led many authorities to conclude that the most practical policy is one which unofficially
permits partisan-controlled invasions of government land.*
So long as they are able to approve the choice of a site, and

---

* The special advantages of shantytown settlements for national urban
development are receiving more and more attention recently by recognized
experts in the field. See in particular the writings of Charles Abrams and
John C. Turner. The latter, speaking of the potential of barrio-type colonies
in Peru, says that "socially and quantitatively, even if not architecturally
speaking, the barriadas are, undoubtedly, the most effective solutions yet
offered to the problem of urbanization in Peru." [148], p. 376.

thus prevent valuable industrial or middle-class residential land from being spoiled, the authorities believe that a well-executed invasion relieves them of many of the burdens they would have to assume were they to take direct responsibility for the housing problem. Except for the actual value of the land itself, an invasion costs the government nothing. It is not called upon to develop and administer the settlement, and it is not required to supply architects, contractors, or social workers. Moreover, the government does not become involved in the delicate controversies that develop regarding the distribution of land, the quality of the terrain, and the prices charged by speculators. In addition, since it assumes no responsibility for the barrio's existence, it is not committed to providing community improvements immediately. Most important, perhaps, the government, through its partisan association with the invasion leader, stands to gain considerable support if he convinces the settlers that the party has enabled them to secure their property. The local officials are aware of what most foreign observers fail to recognize—that for the poor, urban land distribution is as vital a political issue as rural land reform.

Early Development

During the first weeks of its life, a barrio hums with activity as the new settlers clear away brush and stumps, haul in construction materials, and build their rancho frames. Groups of men get together to line out a street or remove some rocks so that the water truck can pass. Speculators transact their deals, while other persons set up temporary bodegas on their lots and sell Pepsi-Cola and beer to the workers. Women run about surveying the progress other families are making on their homes. Favor-seekers besiege the leader. The spirit of the pioneer prevails, and the people are exhilarated by the success of their venture. Gradually life begins to settle down, and it is time to consider the needs of the community; word gets around that a *junta* is to be elected.

A barrio junta is a small committee consisting of between seven and nine residents. Its declared function is to represent the barrio before the city officials and try to obtain basic community facilities. Juntas exist or have existed in every barrio. They are considered a natural part of its early existence, as natural as ranchos and dirt roads, the result of the conviction shared by most families that a barrio can realize its role as a new community within the city only when it has an organized body to represent it.

To form the junta a public meeting is called, in the evening or on a Sunday. Representatives from about half of the families attend. They probably have had disappointing experiences with juntas in other barrios: big plans and promises but no results. Nevertheless, most of the families feel that this is a new start and that maybe this time they will get a good junta; consequently they are animated. The meeting is opened by the invasion leader, who is accompanied by several of his lieutenants and probably by two or three important outsiders, often government officials. He talks of the needs of the community, and the men and women of the barrio express their views. There is common agreement that the most urgent are water and electricity. The subject of the junta is then brought up, and one of the principals declares that it must be nonpartisan and ready to "fight for the progress of the barrio." When nominations are called for, the leader is the first to be proposed for the presidency. He is duly elected by a raising of hands, and his lieutenants are then elected to fill lesser offices. The remaining members are undistinguished residents known and liked by a number of families and with no partisan ties. Usually at least two are women. The officers of the junta are typically president, vice-president, secretary, treasurer, secretary of sports, and secretary of culture; the other members are simply called *vocales*.

One of the first functions of the newly elected junta is to decide upon a name for the barrio. Some names reflect nothing more than the humor or imagination of the president. Some make reference to a physical characteristic of the community, such as "Deep Gulch," "The Island," or "The Meadow." Others reflect political ideals: "The Victory," "The Struggle," "Liberty." Many are derived from famous national figures: "Bolívar," "Andres Eloy Blanco," "José Gregorio Hernández." Some merely refer to historical dates, the most popular being "23rd of January" (the overthrow of Pérez Jiménez) .[6]

At this first public meeting, the junta members announce their intention of going to the Municipal Council to inquire about the possibilities of getting water. They mention other projects as well; a school, a dispensary, and a police house are all discussed, and the residents voice their support of them. The people leave the meeting in an optimistic mood; the future looks bright.

A week later, at a second public meeting, the junta reports that the officials have expressed their interest in helping as soon as possible. The wait for results begins. When it becomes obvious that the expected assistance is not forthcoming, more meetings are held at which the junta explains the delays. Gradually the attendance diminishes, and the president stops calling them. This state of inactivity can exist for months or even a few years. Disenchanted junta members drop out and new ones are added. Unless the junta is smart or lucky enough to divert the community's attention from obtaining water to another feasible project, thus justifying its continued existence, it eventually ceases its efforts and fades into retirement or disbands completely. Subsequently, when the prospects for success are better, a new group is formed or the old reemerges.* Although the status of the junta fluctuates

* Daniel Goldrich, in his study with Raymond Pratt and C. R. Schuller of the politics of the urban lower class in Chile and Peru, also observes a close connection between the amount of government assistance and the vitality of the juntas. Generally, he says, "participation in the local association tends to atrophy as the settlement becomes established," but he adds that this is true to a lesser extent in Santiago than in Lima because of the greater amount of help the Chilean communities get from the authorities. [112], pp. 7–8.

The marked change in the character of community life which occurs in the barrios after the early formation period is very similar to that which William P. Mangin notes in his study of the barriadas of Lima. During the first months, says Mangin, there is a relatively high degree of integration among barriada residents who have a sense of "belongingness" and considerable pride in achievement. Later an atmosphere of impersonalism begins to set in, internal tensions increase, complaints about neighbors are heard more frequently, party politics intervene more often in the community association—which in turn loses respect and power. [127] in [115], pp. 549–550.

depending upon its usefulness, this is not always the case with the individual junta members. While leadership is formally identified with the juntas, it is not always dependent on them. As we shall see, in a number of instances the personal prestige of individual leaders * is sufficiently well established to ensure their dominance in barrio affairs even when the juntas are defunct.

It is almost inevitable that a new barrio fails to get government assistance at least during its first year. Many barrios have been waiting several years for attention; all of them periodically petition the municipal offices, and were a wholly new community to receive help, it would create bitter antagonism. Furthermore, premature assistance to a new barrio would amount to official recognition, thus giving to the invasion an aura of legality. From the point of view of most government representatives, that would be impractical.

The first major physical improvement which the government usually provides is electricity. Electric power is relatively abundant, and the poles and cables can be installed easily and quickly. Next is street repair. Filling and levelling are constantly required during the rainy season, and the city government can offer immediate relief at little expense. Water, which the residents consider their most urgent need, is usually the last of these three improvements to be supplied. There are several reasons for this: water pipe is expensive and in short supply in Venezuela; many cities' supply of potable water is extremely low; and hilly terrain makes the installation of pipe all but impossible in some areas.

Sometimes the delay in obtaining water has salutary consequences. First, desire and frustration heighten appreciation, and this, in turn, stimulates the residents to work together for their own benefit. Occasionally this willingness corresponds with the government's need and desire to economize, so that

---

* The term "leaders" is used in this discussion and throughout the study to refer to the men and women who are dominant figures in community affairs. A "leader" in this sense does not necessarily have the ability to "lead." In fact, as we shall see later, most of them are supported by only a small proportion of their neighbors, the majority being either indifferent toward them or, for personal or partisan reasons, antagonistic.

joint efforts are worked out whereby the government agrees to supply the pipe and the technical assistance, and the community agrees to supply the labor. This cooperative action on the part of community members is known among lower class Venezuelans, in both the city and countryside,[7] as a *cayapa*. A cayapa is usually a spontaneous movement that results when a community believes that a major physical problem can be solved through its own efforts. Since the enthusiasm and spirit of cooperation which give a cayapa its momentum are generally short-lived, its effectiveness is limited, and it usually disbands as soon as its goal is realized, if not sooner. Whereas a cayapa can usually complete a job that requires only a Sunday or two of work, such as installing a water system or repairing a road, it cannot complete a more difficult job that requires months of planning and labor, such as building a school or laying an extensive sewer system.

Barrio residents consider the next most important physical improvement, after the three already mentioned, a school. However, owing to the expense and the time required to construct one, the proportion of communities that still go without is very high. Other physical improvements for which there are varying degrees of demand are asphalting for the streets, street lights, police stations, drainage systems, stairs, and bridges. Occasionally some of these have been provided by municipal and state governments.

Government assistance can also come in the form of services. The Ministry of Education staffs the barrio schools with teachers, and the Ministry of Health and Social Assistance has a program designed to improve barrio health standards. Although as yet it reaches only a small number of communities, the program provides hot lunches to children in school and distributes milk daily to children under six years old. It has also provided some communities with a medical dispensary, and in others it has experimented with a latrine-construction campaign which calls for the ministry to supply the materials and the rancho owners to supply the labor.

Officially Settled Barrios

Not all barrios are formed by invasions. A small number have been officially settled by government authority through a process similar to what Abrams terms "urban homesteading." [8] This process is most consistently used in Valencia, where a special office attached to the Municipal Council and in charge of land distribution appoints a barrio resident affiliated with the governing party to take responsibility for distributing lots within a selected area, without charge, to individual families whose names are officially registered. The fact that lots are given only to registered families and that permission to sell one's parcel must be granted by the government office make speculation more difficult. The direct government involvement also tends to alter the barrio's political life, since the leader appointed to distribute the parcels is endowed with formal authority which reinforces his power in the barrio and his control over its affairs. In an officially settled barrio, the residents are likely to interpret the government's involvement as a sign that it has assumed greater responsibility for barrio problems and, as a consequence, they count even more heavily than independently settled communities on official assistance. In most other respects, however, barrios of this type are developed in the same manner as those discussed previously.

4

The Impact of Modernization on Political Attitudes and Barrio Leadership

Close observation of the barrio people reveals that as they are increasingly affected by the process of modernization taking place in their various cities, social and economic differences develop among them which are distinct enough to divide them into two classes.* This division is clearly reflected in their political attitudes and in the types of leaders that emerge from among their ranks. This development can best be understood when seen against the backdrop of Venezuela's recent political history.

Prior to the death of Juan Vicente Gómez in 1935, local and national politics in Venezuela were controlled by the landowners and the military, and the concept of political authority that prevailed in Venezuela was derived from rural traditions. This concept, which had been nurtured for generations by the *caudillos* and *hacendados,* equated political authority with power, and this, in turn, was based on personal and familial prestige, extensive landholdings, and, when necessary, force.

With the relaxation of political control which followed

---

* "Subclass" would be the more accurate sociological term, but since that would be somewhat cumbersome to repeat continually, especially in a lay discussion of this nature, the shorter term "class" will be used throughout.

Gómez' death, new social groups, often referred to as the middle sectors,[1] emerged to challenge the dominance of the traditional elites. They were essentially the product of the cities, and they sponsored a new and distinctly urban political philosophy—that government should serve the interests of the governed and be based on the will of the people. Their will, in turn, should be expressed at elections in which all adult citizens could participate. The new philosophy also preached that political parties were the best instruments to organize and represent the people's interests and that they should therefore be allowed to operate and mobilize support.

The middle-class political leaders soon directed their attention to the vast lower-class population who had traditionally been excluded from political processes and who had accepted, out of custom, the concept of authority passed on to it by the traditional elites. These leaders sought both the votes and the active participation of the populace in their parties. However, while they made much headway toward ending the political isolation of the poor, they did not at first affect lower-class understanding of political authority. When the poor became the object of the parties' proselytizing, most of them were still residing in the countryside. As campesinos, all of whom lived under the same economic conditions and related in a common way to their environment, they constituted a fairly homogeneous sector of society with deeply rooted traditions. Therefore, instead of transforming the established concept of authority based on power, the parties tended to modify their own practices to resemble those that prevailed in the countryside. The fact that one party, Acción Democrática, had built up an enormous advantage over the other parties and enjoyed unrivalled dominance of rural politics in most areas (where it did not, as in the Andes, another party, COPEI, reigned supreme) greatly facilitated the task of familiarizing the peasants with the party system, since its monopoly of power was not unlike that previously enjoyed by the landowners and the military. As a result, while there can be no doubt that the introduction of the party system into rural areas substantially altered the campesinos' awareness of what they could expect and demand from the government and gave them a totally new appreciation of their role in national politics,[2] it did little to change their day-to-day understanding of the mechanics of the political process and to engender in them a new sense of authority based on popular mandate.

It was not until the campesinos migrated to the cities and encountered the modernizing influence of the urban environment that their homogeneity as a sector of society began to break down; the values as well as the interests of many migrants began to change, and one can now say that they have divided into two classes. One class, much the smaller of the two, has made a conscious effort to adopt the mores of the city and, by doing so, has rejected much of its rural background. The other has retained the essential characteristics of this background and has been only superficially affected by its new environment. An anthropologist's observation regarding the rancho community in which she lived for over two years aptly applies to the whole barrio sector: "My barrio contained not a single class, but the beginnings of at least two levels—a stable working class and/or lower-middle class, and an unskilled and 'imprudent' lower class. The layering of these two levels was incomplete; in my barrio, they were next-door neighbors and even members of the same extended family groups, for the transformation was still very recent. But the difference in style of life was already clear." [3] For the purpose of the study, we shall call the two classes the "aspiring" class and the "general" class.

The Aspiring Class

Representing between 10 and 25 per cent * of the families in each barrio, the aspiring class is identified by its relatively advanced social and economic status, as well as by its more sophisticated political attitudes. Virtually all of its members

* As suggested in the Preface, the estimates of the size of the aspiring and general classes and their respective characteristics are not based on precise statistical data but rather on the author's analysis of a number of community censuses and on his own observations of a great many individual families.

have lived in towns and cities since 1958, many for a longer period of time. They have been able to take advantage of educational opportunities; all of them can read and write, and many have completed six grades. They often read newspapers and can converse comfortably about current affairs. One revealing manifestation of their aspirations is their interest in the English language. Many men have learned words and phrases which they like to use when given the chance; their sons and daughters show a keen interest in attending English classes offered on occasion by North Americans.

Under the current economic conditions, practically all of the men of working age in the aspiring class are employed full-time. Any skilled laborers in the barrios—welders, carpenters, plumbers, and electricians—are of this class. Private industry is generally the most popular source of employment, but there are many who work with government agencies, and others are bodega owners and por puesto drivers. Those who are employed by private industry (or, in the case of the steel industry, by the government) clearly fall into a category which Clark Kerr has called the "generally committed workers." These are men who have "completely severed . . . [their] connection with the village to become . . . permanent member[s] of an urban or industrial work force. This involves more than just being an urban dweller; it requires an adjustment to all the institutional aspects of urban living and industrial employment." [4] In general, the aspiring-class members have a high regard for modernity, organizational techniques, and proper procedure.

The social mores of the aspiring class are similar to those of the established middle class. The family occupies the center of the man's attention. He is concerned about its welfare, especially his children's development; as a result, he usually insists that they attend school beyond the customary three grades. Parents are invariably married, at least by the civil authorities and often by the church as well.* The houses of the aspiring-class members always have cement floors and,

* Gino Germani, in his "Inquiry into the Social Effects of Urbanization in a Working-Class Sector of Greater Buenos Aires" ([107] in [114], p. 216),

when terrain permits, are usually built of concrete or cinder blocks. The women attempt to keep their houses clean, and, as money is accumulated, they purchase household appliances and furniture and make other improvements.

Despite the fairly marked differences between the aspiring class and the rest of the community, these seldom lead to incompatibility among neighbors, for although the aspiring families try to emulate the middle class and strive to achieve its status, they identify with the barrio and make no pretence about their own origins. Perhaps the best evidence of this is the absence of condescension in their attitude toward the rest of the community. While members of the aspiring class, particularly the women, occasionally express distaste for families of the general class, they do not look down on that class as a whole. In contrast, condescension and even contempt are often reflected in the attitude of the middle class toward the barrio people.*

Just as the aspiring-class families readily adopt urban middle-class social mores, they also tend to support the middle sector's political philosophy that governmental authority should be derived from the people's consent. The best evidence of this conviction is the leaders that emerge from among them.**

has also found a close correlation between the proportion of legal marriages and the length of residence in the city among migrants to Buenos Aires. Legal marriage, he concludes, "becomes a symbol of respectability once we take as a reference group not the rural or provincial society itself, which did not regard it as important or necessary, but urban society, which, on the contrary, considers it essential."

* Most barrios have two or three families whose high income and life style put them definitely in the middle class. In contrast to the members of the aspiring class, they have no contact at all with their neighbors. An Italian family in a Caracas barrio, for example, lives behind twelve foot walls guarded by two German Shepherds. Another family sends its son and daughter away to school in the Andes. Their motives for living in the barrios are not clear, although it seems probable that the economic advantage of not having to pay for their land is an important consideration. Because of their negligible involvement in the social and political life of the barrios, they do not merit further mention here.

** The models for the barrio leaders discussed in this chapter are generally men. There are minor variations in the behavior of male and female leaders, but since there are fewer female leaders and since the differences in their behavior tend to be sociological rather than political, it has not seemed worth while to examine them separately for this study. Mention

The typical leader from the aspiring class identifies closely with a system of barrio government that is based on "modern" principles. The system that is well established and generally approved is based on the junta. As an uncomplicated mechanism for community representation, the junta easily satisfies the basic tenets of the political philosophy that the aspiring class has adopted from the middle sector: it is brought into existence by an election, and the authority of its president (the leader) is theoretically derived from the people.

Since the outcome of a junta election is usually the result of political maneuvering by the man who is ultimately elected, such elections are seldom truly representative of the community's will. Nonetheless, the junta president puts much stock in the formal proceedings, for they are the only legal and decisive expression of the people's support that he receives. Similarly, his behavior reflects respect for the institution of the junta itself. When it is necessary for him to identify his role in the barrio, he refers to himself as *"el presidente de la junta,"* and while carrying out the minor tasks that are his responsibility, he generally acts in its name and is careful to solicit the support of at least a few of its members.

Typically, the aspiring-class leader recognizes that his position depends ultimately on his neighbors' willingness to accept him, and he is thus extremely sensitive to public opinion. This is best illustrated by his reaction when faced with dissension in the community. When his actions or proposals are criticized publicly, his customary response is to threaten to resign. While this can be an effective technique for spontaneously consolidating waning support, it is more often a genuine expression of the fear of facing a humiliating loss of prestige. In the event that the dissenting opinion is shared and expressed by a significant number of persons, it can be

should be made, however, of a unique type of female leader one occasionally encounters. She might be called the "barrio mother"; embodying maternal concern for the young, she works continually, and usually alone, to obtain education and sports facilities, playgrounds, and other benefits for the children of the barrio.

assumed that the aspiring-class leader will resign. A barrio in Valencia provides a good illustration. The president of the junta was an alert, progressive member of the locally dominant political party. As the result of his efforts in getting government assistance for the barrio, he won the support of his neighbors and was able to exercise considerable control over community affairs. The extent of his prestige was demonstrated by his success in organizing self-help projects and by the large number of residents who attended the meetings he called to discuss communal needs and problems. This leader was particularly active just prior to the 1963 national elections, and he candidly admitted that the purpose of his work was to gain support for his party. When the election results for his barrio were tabulated, however, the voting proved to be strongly in favor of one of the major opposition parties. Despite the fact that several of his projects were unfinished and that he could be virtually certain of continued dominance over barrio affairs, the leader immediately announced his resignation and withdrew from community affairs.

Although the average leader from the aspiring class is sensitive to public opinion, this does not mean that he is particularly responsive to his neighbors' will, or that he is always an effective leader. Not surprisingly, a man from the aspiring class seeks the junta presidency not because he is primarily concerned with the community's problems but because he desires to fulfill a personal ambition of being recognized as a leader. The potential reward of the presidency is the respect and admiration of his neighbors. Consequently, once having attained his position, he tends to be possessive of it and to protect his authority from any encroachments. This is one of the reasons why the aspiring-class leader is usually domineering and demands to have a say in all matters that might concern the community. The support that he gets from persons outside the community increases his domineering tendencies; these individuals lend him prestige and authority that he often cannot muster on his own. In various barrios this backing has been provided by misguided community-development workers or by well-meaning but indiscriminating priests. More frequently it comes from municipal or state government officials who are anxious to regulate barrio-level politics in the interest either of stability or of their own political parties. Bolstered by this demonstration of official approval, the leader develops an inflated sense of his own importance and attempts to exert increasingly tight control over his barrio's affairs.

The domineering manner of the typical aspiring-class leader reduces considerably his capacity to maintain the support of his community and to perform his function effectively. He easily aggravates his neighbors whose egalitarian pride makes them reluctant to take orders from anybody, and especially from fellow barrio residents. Consequently it is not long before they lose interest in his talk of improvements, and the leader and his junta gradually slip into inactivity.

In exceptional cases men from the aspiring class do demonstrate a larger understanding of their role and are quite effective in developing and maintaining support. Like most barrio leaders, they are attracted to the presidency by the respect associated with the office, but they nevertheless manage to function without letting their self-image hinder their good relations with their neighbors. In group discussions, such a leader tends to speak of "we" rather than "I," and he is anxious to get the opinion of others. He finds real pleasure in seeing things accomplished and has a special liking for projects in which the community as a whole can participate. Although some of these capable leaders are members of a political party, they are careful to keep partisan politics out of barrio affairs and have been known to admonish their friends openly for trying to combine the two. A careful analysis of the background, family relations, and personalities of such leaders might reveal significant differences between them and their less capable counterparts, but there are no obvious distinguishing characteristics.

Among the more effective aspiring-class leaders, the Communist leader deserves special mention. During 1958–1959 he was a strong, and oftentimes dominant, force in many barrios throughout the country, particularly in the central metropolitan area of Caracas and the surounding cities. As in the case of the other exceptional leaders, the Communist maintained support because his neighbors liked the way in which he related to them and what he did for the community. He was generally a friendly, intelligent person; he was dynamic, self-confident, and commanded people's respect. That his beliefs became those of his friends can be attributed more to his charismatic qualities than to their conviction of the validity of his ideology. In his barrio, the Communist made good use of his personal qualities. He became intimately associated with group activities and worked hard for the community's welfare. If anything needed to be done, people learned that he was the man to call on. By sponsoring self-help projects, he tried (especially after Betancourt's inauguration) to foster a spirit of independence from the executive branch of the government and to promote the notion that the community must work because the authorities did not attend to their duties. When the residents saw how successful they could be, they became defiantly proud of their accomplishments, and it was relatively easy for the Communist leader to mold them into little pockets of resistance against the official order. Yet, for the reasons that will be discussed in Chapter 7, the influence of most Communist leaders began to decline after 1959.

The General Class

Between 75 and 90 per cent of the families of every barrio are members of the general class, and it is this group that is largely responsible for the unique culture that one finds in the barrios. Although the great majority have permanently abandoned their country homes and have acquired some new habits and interests, their way of life has not been greatly affected by the urban environment. All recent arrivals begin barrio life in the general class. Nor does one automatically move out of this group with time; there are many general-class members who have been barrio dwellers since the Pérez Jiménez days.

The general-class families are notable for their lack of formal education. For them, unemployment or underemployment is the rule rather than the exception. Of those who do have steady jobs, a high proportion are employed in the public services.* Their allegiance to industrial society is weak, and, in the terminology of Clark Kerr, they can be described at best as "semi-committed workers." [5]

The average income of this group is obviously very low by urban and even by aspiring-class standards. When general-class men do earn a little more than is needed for bare subsistence, they are likely to spend it quickly on fleeting pleasures rather than on benefits of longer duration. The shabby state of their ranchos is the most conspicuous evidence of this habit. In contrast to the aspiring-class adults, those of the general class tend to be content with common-law marriage and are willing to allow their children to grow up with little or no guidance.

Not surprisingly, the political attitudes of this group have not been significantly affected by its urban experience. Most members of the general class still assume that governing power belongs in the hands of those who are able to control it. They do not question the means by which that power may have been attained. Although this group's concept of authority has not changed, members of the general class, like the rural campesinos, do vote, join political parties, and participate in meetings and demonstrations organized by party leaders.** But such activity is not a sign of their adherence to

* Although the problem has not been studied in Venezuela, findings in Italy suggest that one important reason why persons who are most backward and traditional tend to work for government agencies is that they actually prefer to do so. In a survey of some 3,000 Italians between the ages of 18 and 25, it was found that, as one moved southward from the industrialized northern region to the backward southern and insular regions, there was a marked increase in the percentage of those who stated a preference for being employed by a state agency. See [171] in [180], p. 307.

** Unfortunately, hard data on party membership at the barrio level which would enable us to compare the amount of political participation of the general and aspiring classes are not available. It is interesting to note, however, that a survey of the political behavior of the residents of a favela in Belo Horizonte, Brazil ([135], pp. 71–81, esp. Cuadro 5) revealed a correlation between a rise in socio-economic status and an increase in political participation. It would not be surprising, given the evidence we have presented here, to find a similar correlation in the Venezuelan barrios.

the political values of the middle sectors. They are essentially pragmatic in their political allegiance, realizing that with the parties lie the most realistic prospects of satisfying their private material demands and ensuring that the government looks after their welfare.

As in the case of the aspiring class, the political convictions of the general class are most evident in the community leaders that emerge from among its ranks. With very few exceptions, general-class leaders are popularly referred to as *caciques*. Appropriately named after the Indian chiefs who ruled Venezuela prior to the Spanish conquest, caciques represent the supreme, and almost absolute, authority in their barrios. They sanction, regulate, or prohibit all group activities and exercise a strong influence over any decisions that might affect their communities.*

The cacique's authority usually originates with the settling of his barrio and, unless usurped during a time of grave crisis, continues until he voluntarily surrenders it. Either he is the self-appointed head of an invasion, or he has been delegated the responsibility of forming a new barrio by the municipal officials. During the settlement, he maintains strict control over the distribution of parcels. This enables him to establish his reputation as *el que manda* (the one who runs the show) and gives him the opportunity to bestow favors which, in turn, will give him much bargaining power in later dealings with the residents.

Whereas the aspiring-class leader worries about public opinion and his own image, the cacique does not; he acts and

* The close connection between authoritarianism and socio-economic backwardness has been observed by a number of political sociologists (see Seymour M. Lipset's "Working-Class Authoritarianism" in [172] for notes on many of these studies). It is therefore not surprising to find the cacique as a key figure in barrio politics. A study by William J. MacKinnon and Richard Centers, "Authoritarianism and Urban Stratification" [174], has noted a connection between different strata of the U.S. working class and varying degrees of authoritarianism which is remarkably similar to these observations of the situation in Venezuela. The MacKinnon-Centers study describes the results of a survey of 460 persons in Los Angeles County, California, that showed the percentage of authoritarians increased from 51 to 68 to 86 among the skilled, semi-skilled, and unskilled laborers, respectively.

makes decisions affecting other persons without compunction, according to his own judgment. In fact, in a society where self-assurance related to any but strictly personal and family matters is an attribute infrequently found, this is the cacique's most striking characteristic. Moreover, he seems to come by it naturally and, in contrast to his obviously insecure neighbors, he stands solid as a rock, imparting to his people a sense of security.

Various articles written in recent years draw attention to the tendency of the lower-class migrant in Latin America to find a substitute in the city for the traditional authority, *patrón* or *coronel,* on whom he was dependent in the countryside.[6] The authors speak of a clientage arrangement which develops between the new arrival and the "populist" leaders, with the latter appealing to the former's need for government assistance and desire for security in order to build up a large and faithful following. Generally these articles refer to politicians who operate on the municipal, state, or national levels of the political scene and who are members of the middle strata of urban society. However, in the case of the barrio cacique, we have a clear example of such a substitution on the local level, within the migrant's own community.

Unlike the political bosses in the rural areas who gain ascendency over the campesinos but who are not campesinos themselves, the cacique rises out of the midst of the very people over whom he exercises authority. Like most of his neighbors, he has very little money, and he usually lives in a miserable rancho. He is markedly unpretentious and has few of the visible attributes that one commonly associates with political leaders. Conspicuously unconcerned about his dress, he is as likely to receive guests in his home without a shirt on as with.

Nonetheless, he exercises a considerable degree of control over his barrio clientele, as is evident on those occasions when a cacique takes a personal interest in an improvement project being promoted by community development workers and decides to mobilize his neighbors on its behalf. With remarkable ease and on very short notice, he is able to round up twenty to thirty men to work on the construction of a new school or community center.

The cacique asserts his power in subtle ways, and he does not have to be domineering. On the contrary, knowing that the barrio people will not respond to strong-arm tactics, he wins them over with his gregariousness. In Maracaibo, for example, one ambitious man made it a daily practice to wander through his community and stop and chat with the mothers in their ranchos. He was well aware that such outward displays of recognition were cherished, especially by the women, and that his reward would be their faithful support.

Although the cacique is usually the president of his barrio's junta, he has very little regard for it as an institution. When asked to identify his role in the community, the typical cacique replies: "I'm boss around here," or "I'm in charge of this barrio." As if to demonstrate his disrespect, one of Maracaibo's most powerful caciques gave the presidency of his junta to a lieutenant and accepted for himself the meaningless post of secretary so that he would not be bothered by the petty formalities associated with the higher office.

Customarily the cacique enjoys the support of the city's dominant political party. This backing can prove helpful to him in several ways, particularly in coping with problems that concern his authority. For one thing, his rapport with the municipal authorities gives him a quasi-official status that impresses his followers. For another, through his party connections he can find a sympathetic ear in the government offices for his petitions and can get help for community improvements, whereas independent leaders are often at a loss. Finally, should he encounter a serious challenge to his authority, which he is likely to denounce as an "act of subversion," he can intimidate his opponents by threatening reprisal, and on occasion he has arranged to have the police brought in to handle troublemakers.

It is common practice for the cacique to be either fully or partially subsidized by his party or the government. This can take the form of a job or a concession; in a few cases there is no obvious subsidy, but the party lets the cacique use his position to collect money for his own pocket from his neighbors. Because the cacique enjoys this financial support, he is usually able to spend a great part of his time in his own community, keeping a careful watch over its affairs. Consequently, it is hard for potential opponents, especially those from the aspiring class who have outside jobs, to undermine him.

That his position is not completely dependent on official backing has been strikingly illustrated by several cases where a turnover of the municipal government has left a cacique without official support. Instead of selecting a new leader in line with the new government, the barrio residents have continued to follow their old leader faithfully.

The reaction of the cacique when faced with open dissension within his community offers the clearest indication of the difference between his political outlook and that of the aspiring-class leader. Rather than offering his resignation, the cacique consolidates his support and puts up a strong fight. One of the techniques employed to disarm the opposition was demonstrated by a cacique in Maracaibo, who was the president of his barrio's junta and who found his position challenged by an unusually persistent group of neighbors who demanded the election of a new junta. Eventually the cacique had to bow to this pressure, and one night an election meeting was convened. The cacique opened the proceedings with an announcement that the voting would be directed by an "objective" person from outside the community. He introduced the guest, who was well known in barrio circles as an influential member of the city's dominant party. His presence naturally impressed the audience and reminded it of the cacique's contacts. In addition, the guest had brought with him several carloads of party men from neighboring barrios, who stood in the shadows around the outside edges of the crowd. When the time came to vote on the two candidates (the cacique and his challenger), the cacique's name was brought up first. The approval that rang out from the back rows was so boisterous that it swayed many of the potential opposition, who raised their hands. Overwhelmed by this demonstration of power, the challenger was able to muster only a feeble minority.

As this example shows, the cacique, like the military dictator, does not get voted out of office: he either gives up voluntarily or is thrown out. One of the rare instances of the latter alternative occurred when a leader insulted a strong-willed woman of his community and she reported the incident to a city newspaper, which published his picture and a story criticizing him. Since he had been publicly disgraced, it was too late for his party to rescue him, so he left the barrio.

Four Cities

Although we have discussed the characteristics of the leaders who emerge from the aspiring and general classes, we have not as yet discovered why some barrios have one type and other barrios another type, despite the fact that in every barrio, general-class families far outnumber those of the aspiring class. A comparative analysis of the leadership in several different areas clearly indicates that this does not result from a deliberate selection on the part of the community itself. Neither class constitutes an organized group; they both play a more passive than active role in communal affairs. Consequently, the classes rarely assert their particular points of view. More often than not, what determines a barrio's choice of leadership is the economic, social, and political character, as it has developed in the post-war period, of the city in which the barrio is located. In those cities which have remained relatively unaffected by the forces of modernization, and in which the "traditional" character has thus been preserved, leaders from the general class emerge naturally and frequently. However, in cities which have been transformed by the process of modernization, and in which the "traditional" character is rapidly disappearing, aspiring-class leaders, whose political outlook is consistent with the prevailing mood, are able to come to the fore.

The principal features of urban development are most evident in Ciudad Guayana. Although one of the oldest settlements in eastern Venezuela, Ciudad Guayana existed for almost two centuries as nothing more than a quiet village on the southern banks of the Orinoco River.* Then in the late 1940's two large North American steel companies established themselves locally and began to mine the vast iron ore deposits in the nearby hills. As these operations expanded and as the great industrial potential of the region became increasingly obvious, the federal government launched an ambitious, long-range development program and invested heavily in a series of major projects which have thus far included a hydroelectric plant, a steel plant, a large bridge, and dock facilities on the Orinoco River. Attracted by the high-paying jobs that this economic activity created, thousands of families from the surrounding rural areas and (after 1958) from the oil towns of the Oriente, poured into Ciudad Guayana. The town's population increased from a mere 4,000 in 1950 to 100,000 in 1966; by 1975 it is expected to reach 400,000.[7] Given the low economic status of most of the migrants and the lack of housing facilities in the area, it is not surprising to find that the great majority of the newcomers have settled in the barrios.

Heavy industry, represented by the two iron-mining companies and the national steel plant, has played an inordinately important role in setting the pace and tone of the city's development [8] and in shaping the attitudes of the barrio dwellers. To a large extent, Ciudad Guayana's boom-town atmosphere, its aura of dynamism and progress, are the direct result of industry's enormous investment. Its plants and equipment—railroads, tankers, blast furnaces, cranes, and so forth—are the most modern available, and it is by far the largest employer in the area. To the barrio people, heavy industry represents the epitome of advanced technology and efficiency, and this fact does much to explain the prestige that is associated with men who work for the mining companies and the steel plant.

---

* This original village was known as San Félix. With the development of the mining industry in the immediate vicinity, however, several new towns sprang up, the largest of which was Puerto Ordaz. In 1961 the federal government gave the name of San Tomé de Guayana to the greater urban area, but this never caught on, and in 1964 the newly elected Municipal Council adopted the name of Ciudad Guayana.

Although the government, through its development program, has brought profound changes to the city's economy, its influence in the political sphere has been slight until just recently. For one thing, the Corporación Venezolana de Guayana (CVG), the agency created by the federal government to direct the development program, is an autonomous organization whose administrators are appointed in Caracas and which has no party ties with locally based institutions—in particular the Municipal Council. Moreover, all public works projects financed by the CVG have been constructed by various foreign engineering firms. Only since 1964 has the CVG's local administration expanded to the extent that it needs to employ more than just a handful of men from the barrios. In 1963, the CENDES-CIS survey showed that half the people interviewed in Ciudad Guayana had never even heard of the CVG.[9]

Similarly, the activities of the municipal authorities have also been quite limited. Because of the relative unimportance of Ciudad Guayana prior to the advent of the iron-mining industry, the city was not the capital of its district (an administrative subdivision of which there are six in Bolívar state), and it was not given that rank until the end of 1963, when a new district was created out of the former one. Consequently, during most of the period of its rapid growth, the budget allotted to the city by the state capital did not begin to cover its needs, and the expansion of local government activities was therefore precluded by lack of funds. The miniature government office building on the Plaza Bolívar, the unpaved or deteriorating streets, and the total lack of public facilities in the barrios were only a few of the sights that clearly revealed the inability of the local authorities to cope with the city's growth. Other circumstances, especially the tight control of the area's development that the CVG exercised, further inhibited the extension of municipal activities.*

To summarize, Ciudad Guayana represents a rather special

---

* Daniel Lerner, using data collected by the CENDES-CIS survey, emphasizes in his article "Conflict and Consensus in Guayana" [66] in [50]) the high expectations of government held by Ciudad Guayana residents of all income levels. As far as this is true for the barrio sampling, these findings are perfectly consistent with what is manifest in other cities (see Chapter

pattern of development. Its traditional roots have been all but obliterated in a short span of twenty years, during which it has grown from a village to a budding metropolis. This transformation can be attributed to a large extent to the impact of a strong, modern industrial sector. During the same period, the influence of the bureaucratic, public sector has been notably weak.

Under such conditions it would seem probable that a political environment would develop that would support the emergence of aspiring-class leaders. This is in fact the case. While the class itself is still small in relation to the general class, its leadership prevails. Virtually all of the twenty junta presidents in 1964 were from the aspiring class. The majority were employees of the two iron-mining companies and the steel plant. One was a schoolteacher and another a prosperous bodega owner. By and large, these men were not domineering, and this can be attributed mainly to the fact that the government could not sustain an elaborate patronage system to bolster their power within their respective communities. In one case where a leader did try to dictate community politics, he was clearly unsuccessful. This man was "planted" in a barrio by municipal authorities who were worried about the concentration of extreme leftist elements there.* His assignment was to get himself elected president of the junta and thereby to control barrio political activities. To assist him in carrying out his assignment, the municipal authorities gave him the special job of operating the small power plant they had constructed for the community. This served not only to boost his prestige but also to make his assignment financially attractive, since out of the service charges he collected he was allowed to keep a portion for himself. Eventually he succeeded in manipulating his election, and, consistent with his purpose for being there, he tried to run affairs

* The strategy was described to the author by the official who had originally designed it. The leader's own view of his function in the community is noted by Lisa Peattie in [37].

with a very heavy hand. Soon, however, the residents, led by a group of unusually assertive young men, began to voice their complaints and criticism openly, and the leader, reacting like most aspiring-class leaders, surrendered his power.

Moving across the country to Maracaibo, we find a very different political climate from that in Ciudad Guayana. One of the oldest cities in Venezuela, Maracaibo (population: 525,000) has long been the principal urban center of the northwest region. Until 1962, when the bridge over Lake Maracaibo was inaugurated, the city was virtually water-locked from the rest of the nation. This state of semi-isolation helps explain the people's intense regional pride and the fact that theirs is the only major city in Venezuela that has its own distinct dialect. It has also contributed to the develop-ment of strong economic, political, and social institutions that are deeply rooted in tradition.

Despite great changes in its economic structure, Maracaibo has managed to absorb elements of modernity without losing its traditional character.[10] The social and political upheavals of the last quarter-century have been accepted calmly in Maracaibo, without the turmoil and conflict that have been so apparent in Caracas. One reason for this resilience is that the government in both the city and state has been firmly controlled by one political party (except, of course, during the Pérez Jiménez dictatorship).

Most of the migrants attracted to Maracaibo by the eco-nomic activities related to the oil industry came from the interior of Zulia, the three Andean states, and Falcón. All these areas are predominantly rural and are among the re-gions of the country least exposed to Venezuela's postwar industrial growth. Once in Maracaibo, very few of the migrants actually found employment with the petroleum in-dustry itself, since the oil fields were situated a considerable distance from the city proper, the largest ones being on the other side of the lake. Consequently, they had to look for employment elsewhere. This they found either with the numerous peripheral firms that supplied and serviced the petroleum industry, with construction companies, or with

government agencies. None of these organizations helped to
instill in the lower-class workers the spirit of "respectability"
and self-improvement that characterizes the aspiring class.
The firms servicing the oil industry, for example, were small,
highly competitive enterprises whose operations were not
effectively controlled by government regulation. They taught
the poor man not the importance of organization and proper
procedure, but the importance of being shrewd and unscrupulous.

Because of the extent and intensity of the peripheral economic activity that thrived on the oil industry, the post-1958
depression had an especially severe effect on Maracaibo's
economy. Many firms folded, the construction business came
to a standstill, and mass unemployment resulted. It was inevitable that the government sector, whose influence had always been considerable owing to the fact that Maracaibo was
the capital of the state as well as the communications and
marketing center for the region, would assume a more dominant role in the economic sphere. During the first three years
of the Betancourt government, large amounts of federal,
state, and municipal funds were spent in an attempt to alleviate the city's problems; as a result, the government agencies
became by far the largest employers in the city. Patronage,
which had long been a strong tradition, became not only a
political expedient but an economic necessity. Consequently,
it has come to play a central role in the lives of most barrio
families, and they in turn have learned well to understand its
purpose and appreciate its benefits. One needs only to visit
the central Plaza Bolívar any weekday to appreciate this phenomenon. Almost symbolically, facing each other across the
plaza are two of the city's largest buildings, the homes of the
Municipal Council and the State Executive; lining the cor-
ridors or standing in front are the men and women who have
come in from the barrios to get a few hours' work, make a
petition, file a complaint, or just pass the time of day.

Consistent with the principal influences on the city's development, community leadership reveals a high degree of
authoritarianism, with cacique rule almost institutionalized

in a large portion of the barrios. Few members of the aspiring class have had the determination or confidence to try to break these traditions. When they have, they have found their neighbors unresponsive and seemingly unconcerned with the behavior of their supposed representatives.

Ciudad Guayana and Maracaibo are the two cities in which the connection between modernization and political attitudes is most clearly discernible. However, a similar relationship can be seen in Caracas and Valencia.

Although Caracas (metropolitan population: 1,750,000) is an old city in which evidence of its colonial background is still apparent, its present-day spirit is the product of the last fifteen to twenty years. The transformation of the capital began in the the late 1940's and is still going on. From the point of view of the barrio man, the city is undoubtedly Venezuela's supreme example of modernity.* Caracas attracts ambitious families from all over the country because it offers not only opportunities for good employment but also the excitement of a dynamic metropolis. Usually they come to Caracas from other towns and cities (see Chapter 2), and, as a consequence, they are already somewhat acquainted with the ways of urban living.

It is difficult to say whether private investment or government spending has played a greater role in forging Caracas' strong modern image. Certainly both have had an impact. Conspicuous symbols of progress built by the government, such as the super-highways and the federal administration building, Centro Simón Bolívar, have their counterparts in the imposing constructions financed by private enterprise, such as the Shell Building and the buildings of the electric companies and the Creole Petroleum Corporation, and in the ubiquitous and imaginative billboard advertisements.

Since private industry and the government agencies are both heavy employers of barrio residents, neither one has a

---

* The description of Caracas given here applies best to the main, or western, section of the city. In certain respects, the eastern extreme, or Petare as it is called, resembles more the cities of the interior than it does the other sections of the capital.

dominant influence on their values. The advantage that the government could have in this sphere is weakened by the fact that the Municipal Council and the governor's office are controlled by two different parties, and there is thus no one single source of patronage.

Under the influence of the city's vigorous socioeconomic environment, which represents a decisive break with the past and in which the values of the middle sector predominate, a relatively sophisticated political climate has developed in the barrios. In such a climate, the traditional authoritarian rule of the cacique is an anachronism. In order to maintain any degree of support within a community, a leader must produce; if he does not, his neighbors ignore his supposed authority. As a consequence, the rate of turnover of leaders is quite high, and in a number of barrios no one leader has stayed on top for very long. Those men who have succeeded in consolidating positions of real influence almost always are among the best educated, have steady employment, and could be called "good family men." In those cases where powerful leaders do not possess real aspiring-class credentials, as in two barrios in western Caracas, one finds that outside forces have strengthened their hands. In one barrio, it was a community-development organization and, in the other, several influential government agencies.

Valencia (population: 190,000) until quite recently had been a typical provincial capital. Situated in the middle of a fertile valley, the city had traditionally been the chief market for the area's agricultural produce. The orientation of its society was basically rural, and even today many of the most influential families derive much of their income from nearby farms and cattle ranches they own.

Following the overthrow of Pérez Jiménez in 1958, campesinos poured into the city. The new municipal government moved immediately to take control of the settlement of new barrios, and most of them have been formed under official direction. As a result of the municipal government's strong influence on barrio affairs, Valencia is one of the few cities in which there was a high degree of partisan uniformity in junta leadership throughout the Betancourt administration (1959–1964), and, not surprisingly, patronage is quite extensive, although not as pervasive as it is in Maracaibo. In short, the experience of the new barrio residents in Valencia has tended to confirm their traditional understanding of the importance of a strong central authority.

This continuity is being increasingly disrupted, however, by significant changes that are taking place in the economic sphere. The influx of a great variety of private firms, both Venezuelan- and foreign-owned, which began in the late 1950's and gathered momentum after 1960, has transformed Valencia into one of the two or three most important industrial centers in Venezuela.[11] The sudden creation of a large alternative source of employment has started to undermine the influence of the government, and, by putting a premium on occupational skills and education, it has lent additional weight to the values that we have associated with the aspiring class. This development has produced an ambivalent political climate in the poorer communities. As tradition breaks down, so does the influence of the caciques. In 1962, a survey was conducted in a number of Valencia's barrios as part of an official study of the city's industrial and demographic development. One of its findings was that "the definition and choice of [barrio] leaders are based more and more each day on 'technical' criteria. The leader asserts himself more because of his professional qualities than because of his family's prestige."[12] Nevertheless, more than half of the currently recognized barrio leaders still come from the general class, and in those cases where aspiring-class men have come to the fore, with one or two prominent exceptions they have tended to run community affairs with a heavy hand. This has been made possible by the firm backing they receive from the municipal government.

Conclusion

As the evidence in this chapter indicates, one can detect a slow, but nevertheless definite, evolution of the political convictions of the barrio people as they come increasingly under the influence of modernization and industrialization.* While the great majority of the people demonstrate an understanding of political authority that is fundamentally the same as that prevalent in the rural areas, there is a small number of "advanced"—in the socioeconomic sense—members of the barrio sector who are gradually rejecting this traditional concept. Their attitude toward community politics—revealed most clearly by the values and behavior of their leaders as well as by their response or lack of response to these men—indicates that they are affected by "modern" principles insofar as they believe that political authority should be derived from and sustained by popular consent, and that it can justify its existence only to the extent that it serves the people's interests.

This basic change in attitude clearly points to a new political awareness and to a new concept of the proper relation between the governed and their government. It suggests that these individuals are beginning to develop an appreciation of themselves as citizens to whom are owed certain political rights, and that they are becoming more sensitive to a notion of political justice. Thus we can hypothesize that, whereas the demands of the general class are primarily *material*, those of the aspiring class are *material* and *political*. The members of the aspiring class continue to demand water, land, and schools, but they also seek political liberties, equitable treatment from officials, and effective channels through which to voice their grievances.

Were the influence of the aspiring-class members in the barrio sector roughly proportionate to their small numbers,

* Implicit in this discussion is a conclusion which several writers have recently drawn about the nature of the urbanization process in Latin America—that it has a much weaker modernizing effect on the political and developmental attitudes of rural migrants than does industrialization. Urbanization can occur without significant industrialization and where it does, at least in Venezuela, attitudes are not likely to change substantially. See, for instance, Alfred Stepan's interpretation [144] of Joseph A. Kahl's articles [120] and [121]. Richard M. Morse [133] cites an unpublished 1965 study of Brazil, "Patterns of Urban Growth and Their Political Consequences" by Frank Sherwood, who reportedly "found there was not as high a correlation between levels of urbanization and voter eligibility and participation as between these latter and industrialization."

their "advanced" political convictions would not be especially noteworthy. However, as we have seen in Ciudad Guayana and Caracas, if the socioeconomic and political environment of a city is consistent with the values and outlook of the aspiring class, the influence of that class is likely to be dominant.

5

Obstacles to Direct Cooperative Action

One of the prominent features of barrio politics is the extreme infrequency with which residents take the initiative to alleviate common problems through direct, cooperative action. When several of them do resolve to seek improvements, they invariably proceed by making a petition to a municipal or state government office. To be sure, there are occasions when they participate personally in community projects—as illustrated by the cayapas mentioned in Chapter 3—but in almost every such case of collective action it is possible to trace the initiative back to some outside force, such as a government official, party leader, community development worker, or priest. One rarely hears of a group of men, even after they have petitioned unsuccessfully, deciding to tackle by themselves a problem which they consider urgent and then actually going to work. This is true even of minor problems: the residents are just as disinclined to get together to mend a broken water spigot as they are to build their own schoolhouse.

This characteristic is by no means uncommon in lower-class communities of developing countries. On the contrary, it has been frequently alluded to by anthropologists, community development workers, and technical assistance teams who have lived and worked in such communities, especially in rural areas.[1] It is, however, somewhat surprising to find this characteristic so prominent among the barrio residents, for many of the cultural, social, and economic factors that have been cited as obstacles to self-help in other countries are either absent or of little significance in the Venezuelan cities. In fact, in comparison to conditions in other lower-class communities, those in the barrios would seem quite propitious for direct, cooperative action.

In the first place, barrio dwellers are generally well aware of their communities' deficiencies and are anxious for improvements. If an outsider walks into a barrio and asks about local needs, the residents will immediately mention water, electricity, schools, street repair, sewers, and street lights. A longer list of "necessities" is likely to include sports facilities, police protection, sewing classes, and a milk-distribution program. Moreover, the custom of electing juntas and sending requests for assistance to government agencies clearly demonstrates that the people care enough about their communities to exert at least some effort to improve them.

In the second place, the reluctance to take cooperative action is clearly not a consequence of any established cultural values that prevent the people from working together. As the barrio residents have demonstrated by their participation in cayapas and other community activities initiated by outsiders, they appreciate the benefits that can be derived from cooperation and on occasion are willing to try it. This would seem to indicate that the exclusive preoccupation with the nuclear family that has been cited by Edward Banfield and others * as a basic cultural barrier to collective action in rural communities is a factor of relatively little importance in the barrios.

In the third place, in contrast to the situation that exists in other lower-class communities, many of the barrios' problems could be solved with relatively little assistance from the outside. Rancho families are not handicapped, for instance, by

* Banfield, in his study of the political incapacity of the residents of a village in southern Italy (*The Moral Basis of a Backward Society* [160]), attributes a great variety of manifestations of the reluctance to cooperate with one another in matters of mutual interest to "amoral familism," which he says is characterized by the rule of thumb: "Maximize the material, short-run advantages of the nuclear family, assuming that all others will do likewise." For a review of similar findings in other areas see Rogers [181].

the myriad legal and physical obstacles—strict government ordinances, multistory buildings, absence of vacant land, heavy automobile traffic, and their tenant status—which severely limit slum dwellers' opportunities to deal directly with their common problems. Nor are they impeded by the extreme scarcity of material and technical resources that is characteristic of peasant settlements. Their urban environment, with its social and economic advantages, enables the rancho families not only to raise money through collections, raffles, and bingo games, but also to count on the services of skilled laborers, such as masons, carpenters, electricians, and seamstresses, who are living within their barrios. A rare example of genuine community self-help illustrates well how effectively the barrio dwellers can take advantage of the opportunities for cooperative action that are open to them, if they are so inclined. A leader in a barrio of Maiquetía and a group of his neighbors decided to establish a community school after they realized that the government was unable to provide one. They located and renovated an old abandoned rancho, built benches and blackboards, petitioned for schoolbooks, and then selected from among themselves teachers for the first six grades. Several months after a jubilant inauguration, the school was officially registered by the Ministry of Education.[2]

Finally, there exist in most barrios recognized leaders whose principal function, at least in theory, is to seek relief of communal problems and thus to provide the very initiative we are discussing. Moreover, the government and party officials provide the incentive that a leader may need to perform his function; anxious to win popular support, they will reward any leader who shows that he can successfully mobilize and direct his people.

Why, despite these apparently favorable conditions, do barrio dwellers so infrequently take the initiative to work together for their common good? Probably the most meaningful explanation can be found if we contrast their behavior with that of the campesinos. As a group, the campesinos are less sensitive to their own problems, they have less motivation and fewer resources to solve them, and, as a result, they rarely initiate group activities. However, when they are lent the outside assistance necessary to undertake a community project, they are markedly more inclined to cooperate with one another. This has been clearly revealed by the experience of community development workers, who have found organizing large self-help projects, such as the construction of a school or community center, and seeing these through to completion, much simpler tasks among campesinos than among barrio dwellers. It is not necessary to go into the countryside to notice this striking difference in behavior. It was convincingly demonstrated, for example, in a barrio on the outskirts of Maracaibo, in which the older campesino element was dominant. In 1964, a large group of residents, with the help of a community development worker, resolved to build a school which would satisfy their entire community's needs. Relying on construction materials provided by private companies, but contributing all the labor themselves, they were able, after only ten months of working just on Saturdays and Sundays, to open a six-classroom school, complete with living quarters for the principal and separate bathrooms for boys and girls.

When we look for the factors that best account for this difference in behavior and attitudes, one seems especially relevant: the campesinos have a much greater sense of security regarding their place in society and their relationship with their peers.[3] For generations their economic and social roles have been essentially constant. They grow up with a good understanding of what they can expect from society and what they must give to it. They know their neighbors well, either because they are related or because they have lived nearby for years. Everyone is familiar with the social customs and regulations. For the campesinos, life is routine and generally predictable. As a consequence, they are not overly inhibited in their relations with their peers and can be induced with relative ease to cooperate on matters of common interest. By contrast, the barrio dweller lives in an environment which is complex and unreliable. He lacks social as well as economic security. He does not know his neighbors and cannot predict their motives, opinions, and reactions. The description that Clark Kerr has offered of the typical effects of industrialization and urbanization on the migrants in developing countries applies to the psychological impact of the transition that barrio dwellers have undergone: "The wrenching from the old and the groping for the new in the industrial community creates a variety of frustrations, fears, uncertainties, resentments, aggressions, pressures, new threats and risks, new problems, demands and expectations upon workers-in-process, their families and work groups." [4] More specifically, one of the critical differences between rural and urban life is the degree to which the poor are exposed to the activities, rivalries, and conflicts of political parties. Whereas the struggle between the government and the political organizations of the extreme left has been witnessed by only small numbers of campesinos, it has been almost a daily experience for most barrio residents. Similarly, the latter have had much more contact with community leaders who attempt to influence barrio affairs and secure advantages for themselves and their political parties. A good indication of the psychological effect that these experiences and the general uncertainty of urban living has had on those who have migrated from the countryside is provided by the CENDES-CIS survey [5] which shows that, whereas the campesinos are ranked more trusting than half of the groups interviewed, barrio dwellers are ranked the least trusting of all.*

While the latter's sense of insecurity is not apparent in their private behavior—they are still extraordinarily independent as individuals and are unaffected by what others may

---

* The ranking of the groups was based on their choice between the proverbs, "Trust in people and you will go a long way," and "Never trust anyone but yourself." Unfortunately the knowledge of the present writer and the limits of this study prevent us from doing any more here than drawing attention to the striking contrast between the behavior and attitudes of the Venezuelan peasant and of those who were the object of studies by Foster. Foster ([166], p. 51) concludes that ". . . to a greater or lesser extent peasant life is characterized, within the village, by a bitter quality of mutual suspicion and distrust which makes it extremely difficult for people to cooperate for the common good."

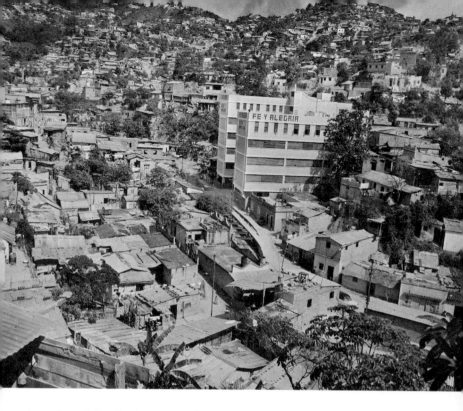

A section of barrios in eastern Caracas. Large building
in center is one of a number of schools built for barrio children by a
private philanthropic organization, Fé y Alegría. *Accion en Venezuela*

Sections of two barrios on crowded
hillsides of Caracas.   *M. Agar*

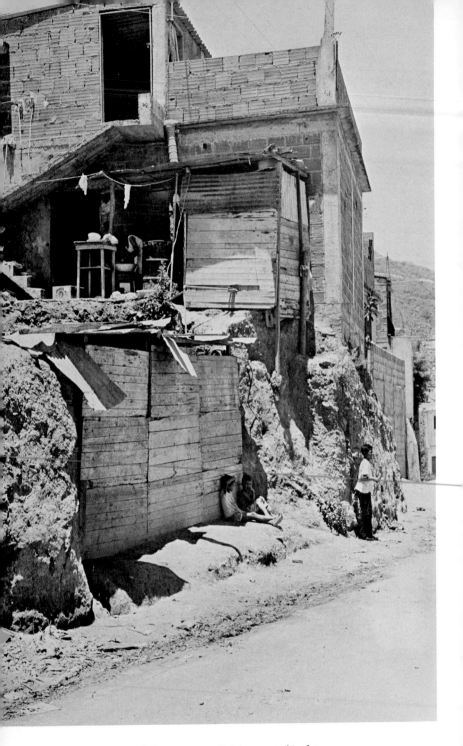

Families crowd into any available space in the
barrios of central Caracas.

José Sigala

Barrio in extreme western end of Caracas.
Long distances from public facilities and transportation diminish
demands for rancho sites here, permitting sparser settlement. *Noguera*

A Maracay barrio as it appeared
just after invasion.   *T. F. Ray*

Invasion leaders, equipped with surveying pole and steel measures, discuss where to locate a street.

M. Agar

Two families secure their claims to parcels of land in a newly formed barrio in Maracaibo by erecting two poles and stretching out their hammocks.

T. F. Ray

A family settles into its provisional home on
recently invaded land in Maracaibo.   *T. F. Ray*

Men and children of a hillside barrio in Caracas cooperate, cayapa style, to build much-needed stairs.

Accion en Venezuela

A committee chosen from among neighbors visits the office of a government agency to explain its barrio's needs and to request assistance.

Accion en Venezuela

The proud mother of an "aspiring class" family, sits beneath
diplomas and certificates earned by members of her family. A picture
of her son, a high-school student, stands in cabinet. *José Sigala*

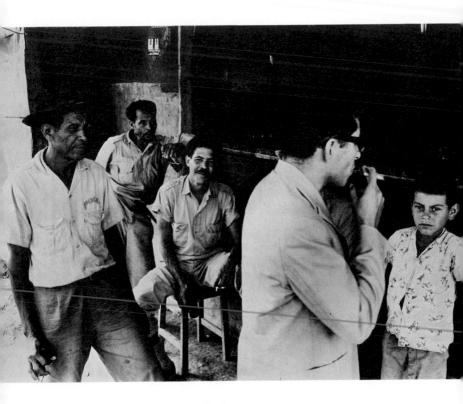

Men drinking beer at a bodega,
the barrio's main site for social contact.

José Sigala

think of their morals and dress—it is clearly evident in their public behavior. The experience of community development workers reveals that this characteristic is perhaps the most formidable obstacle to direct, cooperative action in the barrios.* One manifestation of this insecurity is the unwillingness of barrio dwellers to work on community projects unless accompanied by a number of their neighbors. Afraid to be caught working alone while others are watching, they wait to begin until they are sure that several neighbors will be joining them. This, incidentally, is why workdays usually do not get started until late in the morning, although the men get up very early and have nothing else to do in the meantime.

This hesitation is just as conspicuous among leaders, particularly those of the aspiring class. Generally at the beginning of a project they avoid assuming any significant responsibilities and, when pressed on this point, attribute their inactivity to the shortcomings of their neighbors, usually remarking that "The people are too lazy," or "They don't want to work." Later when the project is under way, when the chances of success appear good and the major risks have been eliminated, these same men suddenly become active and start giving directions to others. However, should trouble develop, or should they become the object of criticism, they again betray their feeling of inadequacy. Then, as we have noted, their usual tendency is to resign, or threaten to do so. Robert Scott's analysis of the psychological barriers to political participation among Mexicans applies very well to Venezuelan aspiring-class leaders. He writes: "The lack of a feeling of personal effectiveness affects political competence. Although the sense of inadequacy is masked behind a façade of high cognitive self-appraisal, the performance of most persons in the political process is consistent with their deeper self-image.

* Jack Mezirow, writing of the community development program among Pakistani villagers ([175], pp. 197–202), says that even when one of them "becomes aware of a problem and is interested in its solution, it does not necessarily follow that he will actively become involved in an action project designed to attack it." Of the ten reasons he offers to explain this behavior, no less than seven are closely related to fear, insecurity, and uncertainty.

The sense of and desire for dependency encourage relation to the output function; the sense of inadequacy reduces evaluation of self as a political actor and limits participation on the input side." [6]

The importance of self-confidence among the leaders as a prerequisite for direct action is underlined by the fact that it is the caciques who, when they perceive a definite benefit for themselves, are most likely to take the initiative. In a Maracay barrio, for example, a cacique owned a bodega situated near the road, which was crossed by a ditch. During the rainy season, the ditch would flood and prevent the delivery truck from reaching his store. Because this situation was a personal inconvenience to the cacique, he requested a donation of materials from a local religious organization, organized his friends and political supporters, and constructed a bridge, thus eliminating the problem.

As might be expected, the reluctance of the people to work together increases as they learn more about the risks involved. In 1958, when barrio dwellers were celebrating the restoration of political liberties following the overthrow of Pérez Jiménez and shared the mood of trust and solidarity that prevailed among those who supported the Provisional Government, they were willing to experiment with cooperative action and undertook various community projects, particularly in Caracas where the Plan de Emergencia made materials available for improvements. Later, however, when the political parties began to look after their own interests and compete for dominance, and when unscrupulous leaders began to take advantage of such projects for private gain, disenchantment and cynicism set in and the barrio people became steadily less willing to give up their time and energies for what they thought would be the benefit of others. The same change in attitudes can be noted during the early stages of the life of an individual barrio. In a Maracaibo barrio, for instance, a team of community development workers found that the greatest problem they had in developing interest in a community center was not apathy but the widespread belief that they were associated with the former junta president. Three years previously he had stirred up much enthusiasm for the construction of a school, self-help style, and, after collecting a large sum of money from the community under the pretext of buying the necessary materials, he abandoned the barrio and built a new home for himself in another part of the city.

The lack of confidence that is characteristic of most barrio dwellers, particularly vis-à-vis their political roles, is further manifested in their diffidence toward "authority," a nebulous concept whose presence is always felt in the barrios. Authority is usually identified with government officials and is sensed as much by the leaders as by the people in general. However, where juntas are strong and government-supported, they can also represent authority to the rest of the community. Well aware that authority is capable of causing them damage, people are very reluctant to take any public action that might offend it. When confronted with such an opportunity, they reveal their concern with remarks like "We must ask permission," "That wouldn't be proper," or "It must carry the junta's stamp." The conventional and accepted method for dealing with community needs is the petition, and people are afraid to try new approaches, such as direct action, lest they be reprimanded by some figure of authority. Even leaders associated with the locally dominant party conform so as not to appear to be stepping out of line. Although this diffidence is a carry-over from many years of lower-class subservience to authority and is, therefore, basically intuitive, it has been aggravated in recent years by the intense struggle, especially acute during the Betancourt administration, between the government and antigovernment political parties and by the officials' extreme sensitivity toward any political activities that might constitute a threat to stability or to their power.

Given this prevailing sense of insecurity, it is not surprising to find that cooperative action is usually initiated by persons outside the barrios. Lacking sufficient confidence in themselves, barrio residents need the reassurance of persons or institutions whom they respect as authority figures that their actions will not bring them more harm than good. On occasion this assurance is provided by community development workers, priests, or, in Caracas, opposition party leaders, but most often it is provided by persons associated with the municipal or state governments. In other words, unless their actions are officially sponsored or authorized, few barrio men have the confidence to organize themselves and their neighbors in order to realize a common goal.

The only organizations that have been able to get large numbers of barrio people to act in concert for political purposes have been the government agencies, the labor unions, and the political parties; and in the interior cities (that is, in every city except Caracas), this capacity has been limited almost entirely to those organizations affiliated with the local governing authorities, while the local opposition parties have been unable to mobilize their barrio followers.* In these cities, street demonstrations and invasions are organized almost exclusively by men who are linked, through partisan ties, to the municipal and/or state governments. The importance of such links as a prerequisite for popular mobilization is illustrated by the Puerto Cabello rebellion of 1962, which was the most violent demonstration against the national government since the Revolution of 1958. Two parties of the extreme left (PCV and MIR) inspired the rebellion, and although they were not actually participating in the municipal government, they were informally allied with the party (URD) which controlled the Municipal Council and which at that time was in militant opposition to the national government. Moreover, the majority of barrio residents who took part in the fighting were from one large barrio whose popular leader was an official in the municipal government and an influential member of the URD party. Although the municipal government did not publicly sanction the rebellion, it is very doubtful that the barrio people could have been so

---

* The one exception occurred at the time of the Revolution of 1958, when the parties which were opposed to the Pérez Jiménez regime were successful in mobilizing the barrio sector. This success, however, was owing to the special political conditions that existed at the time and which will be discussed in Part III.

easily persuaded to participate had they not realized that the local authorities were at least spiritually behind their cause.

The nongoverning parties in Caracas have demonstrated considerably greater ability than those in the interior cities for getting barrio dwellers to act collectively. The best example of their accomplishments is the Revolution of 1958, but they have also been the principal force behind various mass demonstrations, transport strikes, and other similar activities in which barrio people have participated. One obvious reason for this greater degree of politicization is that Caracas is the center of national politics and the headquarters of all the major political parties, whose leaders consider the populous capital crucial to their interests and spend more time and money there trying to build up their influence. Also, as we have noted, Caracas has generally attracted the better educated, more ambitious, and more alert members of the lower class, many of whom have lived in other cities before moving to the capital; and it is in Caracas that the influence of the aspiring class is most profoundly felt. The barrio people of Caracas tend, therefore, to be more sensitive to their political rights and quicker to nurture and express political grievances —and to have much less respect for authority—than their counterparts in areas where the general class is dominant. Consequently, when backed by ambitious and energetic opposition parties, they are more willing than most barrio dwellers elsewhere to take collective action that runs counter to the interests of the government.

6

The Government's Role
in the Barrios

The subject of government involvement in barrio affairs has recurred several times in this discussion, specifically in connection with the formation process and the installation of community facilities, the support it gives to aspiring- and general-class leaders, and the initiation of direct, cooperative action in the barrios. Directly or indirectly, government officials play a very important role in the dynamics of barrio politics. In this chapter we shall examine more closely the people's understanding of this role, how the understanding has developed, and how it affects their political attitudes.

The officials with whom barrio residents come in contact derive their authority directly, or indirectly by appointment, from the national elections held once every five years. When the Venezuelans go to the polls they cast two ballots. The major one, the *tarjeta grande,* is cast for a presidential candidate, and a simple plurality determines the President of the Republic. He appoints the governors of the twenty states, two federal territories, and one federal district. They are his personal representatives, and they, together with the staffs they appoint, administer the national programs at the state and municipal levels. The governors also appoint the district *prefectos,* who are responsible for law enforcement at the municipal level.

The second ballot, the *tarjeta pequeña,* is cast for a political party. Proportionate to the number of votes received by the individual parties at the state, district, and municipal levels, those parties delegate representatives to the two houses of the National Congress, the state assemblies, and the municipal councils respectively. Of these three governing bodies, only the municipal councils directly affect barrio affairs. Depending on the size of the city they have either seven or nine members, who usually represent two or three parties. The council president is elected by the members, and, except when special compromises are required, is the leader of the majority party. He is responsible for appointing municipal officials.

From their vantage point at the lowest level of urban society, barrio residents develop a rather special understanding of government. As they see it, government has two principal functions. In practice, however, these functions are incompatible with one another, as we shall see.

Probably the most general view among barrio residents is that the government is supposed to provide the keys to their social and economic advancement. Not only *can* it supply most of the benefits of urban life—jobs, educational facilities, running water, diversions, transportation, and so on—but it *should* supply them.* The extent to which they are convinced of this is illustrated by several bizarre examples. When the Orinoco River flooded in 1962, rancho owners in Ciudad Guayana and Ciudad Bolívar held the Ministry of Public Works responsible. During a recent invasion in Maracay, a man set up his little hut in a dry creek bed; shortly afterwards, when the rains came and swept it away, he demanded that the Municipal Council build him a new home on a better parcel. When the price of milk goes up, barrio youths are among those who march through the streets of Caracas carrying signs condemning the government. Women blame

* This characteristic has often been publicly recognized and lamented by high government officials. For example Betancourt, referring to the national community development program, said in a speech delivered at Teatro Nacional, Caracas, January 15, 1964, that the program had been introduced "in order to eradicate the paternalist conception of the Government and the State from the minds of the Venezuelan people, whose expectations were all centered on action by the State." (Quoted in [153], p. 232.)

the local officials when the meat at the market is bad or when water at the fountain is cut off because of repairs. When a boy drowns at a forbidden swimming area, the authorities are condemned for not providing a lifeguard.

The inclination to depend on help from above is not new; it is an integral part of the heritage of the barrio dwellers. In fact, the municipal and state governments could be considered merely the latest in a long succession of institutions— beginning with the Indian caciques, who ruled Venezuela prior to the Spanish conquest, and continuing through the caudillos and the hacendados [1]—to whom the poor man has traditionally looked for protection and succor.[2] But in the city the bonds of dependency are strengthened out of economic necessity. Most men in the barrios do not have land enough to cultivate, nor do they have the ability, experience, or money to establish a business of their own (see Chapter 2). Consequently, in order to sustain themselves and their families, they must find a job. As we have seen, however, the supply of jobs for the uneducated and unskilled, relative to the demand, is very small. The government agencies have recognized this problem and have attempted to alleviate it by creating new jobs especially designed for barrio dwellers in construction or as street cleaners, night watchmen, and so forth. Because such work is irregular and the levels of productivity are low,[3] the government has succeeded only in moving from a state of severe unemployment to one of widespread underemployment. Nonetheless, the fact remains that many persons who previously earned no money are now earning an income, and, as a consequence, a large number of families has come to depend upon the government for their livelihood.

This sense of dependency is strengthened by the great need for community improvements and by the barrio dwellers' knowledge that the government is the only source on which they can rely to any significant degree for outside assistance. Private firms, for the most part, have not yet ventured into the barrios on a business basis; the much-heralded housing project of one of Venezuela's leading industrialists, for instance, is geared to lower-middle class needs and does not touch the barrio problem.[4] Only the electric companies that provide service to barrios in Maracaibo, Barquisimeto, Valencia, and part of Caracas help alleviate the government's burden. Similarly, the private social programs that are active in some urban areas have affected only a tiny portion of the barrio population. A third source of assistance could be the barrio dwellers themselves, but, as we have noted, they are reluctant to resort to their own resources to meet communal needs.

Although these factors do explain the barrio dwellers' dependency on the government, they do not explain their conviction that they are justified in demanding as much as they do from the government. This conviction can be attributed chiefly to the enormous influence that the words and actions of the middle-class political leaders have had on the barrio people's political attitudes, convincing them that the principal duty of responsible government is to look after the welfare needs of the poor. This notion of government has been fostered by the parties since the earliest days of their activities, in the early 1940's, when they went out in pursuit of the electoral support of the Venezuelan populace. The government itself lent some substance to this notion from 1945 to 1948, when it attempted to carry out far-reaching social and economic reforms. However, the Revolution of January 1958 and the political activities that followed in its wake were responsible more than anything else for embedding this conviction in the minds of the barrio residents.[5] Carried out in the name of "the People" and with the active participation of the barrio dwellers (see Chapter 8), who had been almost entirely ignored by the Pérez Jiménez regime, the Revolution was proclaimed to have ushered in a new era in which the demands of the urban poor would be well attended to. The Provisional Government, led by Wolfgang Larrazábal, went far in fact to live up to the hopes that the events of January 23 had created. Anxious to satisfy neglected demands, it openly permitted the settlement of barrios, especially by invasion, installed many community facilities, and handed out

jobs. Because of these benefits, many barrio dwellers, particularly in the major cities of central Venezuela, still look back to
1958 with nostalgia, hoping for the return of a government
equally attentive to their interests.

A revealing illustration of the expectations created by the
Revolution was the shocked reaction of the superbloque
dwellers when they were asked in late 1958 by the adminis-
trating agency (the Banco Obrero) to pay rent on the apartments they had invaded immediately following the January
overthrow of Pérez Jiménez. For many the free use of the
superbloques represented one of the major victories of the
Revolution, and to be denied that was to be denied one of
their legitimate rights as lower-class citizens.[6] Although the
political life in the superbloques was dominated by Communists during this period, the reaction of the dwellers as a
whole should not be interpreted simply as a tactic of the
extreme left to embarrass the government. It was much more
likely a genuine expression of the dwellers' concern that the
revolutionary ideals as they understood them were being
abandoned.*

The period following the Revolution was a particularly
active one politically, and the parties, through their proselytizing, continued to play a key role in forming the popular
image of governmental responsibilities. Almost immediately
after the victory of the Revolution was celebrated, the parties
launched an election campaign which was to be the first open
contest of its sort since 1947. In that campaign, three presidential candidates competed with one another, each trying to
offer the barrio dwellers the assurance that a government run
by him would represent the best hope for their advancement.
By 1963, the year of the next presidential election, the
barrios had grown even more populous, and leaders from
seven parties expended the greatest amount of their oratorical
energy on promises for social improvements that would primarily benefit that sector: the creation of hundreds of thousands of new jobs, massive federal programs for urban re-

---

* Because of the strong popular resistance, agency efforts to get the
superbloque dwellers to pay rent were largely frustrated until about 1963.

newal, expanded facilities for recreation, and campaigns to eradicate misery and hunger. Even the party (COPEI) that traditionally received most of its support from the middle class had as the central plank in its platform the pledge to build 100,000 homes for the lower class during *each* of the five years of its administration.[7]

What the barrio people have not learned about the responsibilities of government from the parties, they have learned from personal experience with the officials themselves. In sharp contrast to the stereotyped image of the Latin American official who stands aloof from the activities of the lower-class citizens, government officials in Venezuelan cities have as much personal contact with this sector as possible. They leave their doors open to petitioners and receive them warmly. A request for assistance is never flatly refused; even in the most negative response there is always some room for hope. Officials frequently visit the barrios, attending inaugurations of improvement projects, sports events, and junta meetings. In some cities, mayors and even state governors take Saturday excursions through the poorer communities and talk with the people about their problems. This contact with the urban poor is very important to the officials: on the one hand, it keeps them abreast of the people's political tendencies; and, on the other, it gives them exposure to the families whom they must persuade to vote for them. Obviously the strategy does not always accomplish its purpose—to be effective it must be backed by action—but it does serve to confirm the barrio man's belief that his welfare and the government are intimately linked.

As we have noted earlier, the dependency of the barrio sector on the government creates problems for the officials insofar as they are held responsible for many of the ills of barrio life. This drawback, however, does not manifest itself in any notable inclination of the officials to alter the relationship by encouraging greater independence. In fact, many conscientious officials are likely to be distressed when they hear about projects being carried out without their involvement. To them it is a sure sign that they have not been on their toes. Their reaction is either one of embarrassment, in which case they hurry in with unrequested aid, or one of anger at the effrontery of barrio leaders or of community development workers, for initiating a project without their knowledge.

While the people have grown to rely on the government as their best hope for social and economic advancement, they have also come to realize that it has another, much more exclusive function—namely, to serve the partisan interests of the officials who administer it. In fact, many barrio residents believe that government is really just the instrument of the governing parties.

This view is not peculiar to the barrios. It is prevalent in other sectors of Venezuelan society, and it is an issue that is openly discussed. The governing parties themselves nurture this image as they negotiate for months about the terms for forming a coalition: Who will get which offices? What will the advantages and disadvantages be? Where can power be used most effectively? The opposition parties are constantly accusing the government of using official power for partisan ends, and, as a result, words such as *ventajismo* and *paralelismo* * have been incorporated into popular jargon.

The electoral system makes this controversy almost inevitable. Since Congressmen, state assemblymen and municipal councilmen are all put into office because people voted for their respective parties but not for them as individual candidates, it is natural that these representatives, and the officials whom they in turn appoint (particularly on the local level), should demonstrate allegiance to their parties in handling authority.

The Venezuelan fiscal system also contributes to the emphasis on party ties. Only a tiny portion of the revenue that

---

* *Ventajismo* is derived from *ventaja*, meaning "advantage," and refers to the use of government power to advance the cause of the governing party at the expense of the opposition. *Paralelismo* comes from *paralelo* and refers to the government's practice of establishing new, "parallel" organizations, such as unions and juntas, to rival and undermine existing organizations controlled by the opposition.

pays the officials' salaries and provides the funds for their budgets is derived from personal income taxes; over two-thirds comes from taxes paid by the oil and iron-mining companies.[8] This means that the funds are raised at little or no financial sacrifice to the average Venezuelan family. Recognition of this fact does not alter, of course, the government's legal and moral responsibility to distribute expenditures without political discrimination, but it does help foster the attitude that outlays of government funds are gifts which are bestowed on the public—as opposed to obligations owed to it—and, as such, can be distributed to beneficiaries of the officials' choosing.

While other sectors of society are aware in a general way of the partisan use of authority, the barrio residents are constantly exposed to it. As we have noted, they are heavily dependent on government for assistance in the form of jobs, communal facilities, and education. This dependence, of course, makes them especially vulnerable to the whims of officials who want to manipulate them to serve their own purposes. Not infrequently, officials take advantage of this situation to give preferential treatment to members or strong supporters of their party. Such a practice has already been referred to in connection with the opening up of new land for barrio settlement, and it is also evident in the distribution of both temporary and permanent government jobs. Similarly, there are numerous examples of barrios which have received improvements that are in limited supply—such as water and schools—because of special bonds between their junta presidents and the officials. Leaders are "rewarded" for their ability to create a favorable image of the government among their followers. It was chiefly for this reason, for instance, that a large sports field was recently constructed in a Maracaibo barrio despite the fact that most other Maracaibo communities were still petitioning for schools. In addition, there are cases where assistance to a barrio has been withheld because of its people's allegiance to one of the opposition parties.

That barrio residents are so vulnerable to this type of arbitrary decision-making by the officials can be attributed in part to the absence of any well-defined government programs, or even guidelines, for providing community improvements. Since the officials are not publicly committed to certain plans of action, they are obviously less inhibited than they would be otherwise by the fear that their preferential treatment of supporters will be recognized. Further working to the disadvantage of barrio residents is the petition system which, like the fiscal system, contributes to the attitude prevalent in official circles that the provision of barrio improvements is more a favor then a responsibility of government.

A less obvious but no less common technique is officials' use of the junta system to further the governing party's interests. As we have seen in Chapter 3, not all barrios have juntas at any given time, but virtually all have had at least one at some time since their formation. Their usefulness to the governing party stems from the fact that they are the only community bodies that most barrio residents recognize as legitimate. To the extent that group activities exist with a barrio, the juntas are invariably the center around which they revolve. Communities whose junta presidents are unpopular or ineffectual are notable for the absence of group activities, not for activities that are carried on behind the presidents' backs. It is illustrative of their role that every junta has its own special rubber stamp, and that no petitions for communal improvements are considered valid either by the residents themselves or by government officials unless they bear the stamp's imprint.

Obviously, then, the municipal and state governments benefit if the juntas in their particular city are loyal supporters, since through the juntas the officials are better able to regulate and control the political life of the barrios. The existence of such juntas helps ensure that all political activity in these communities has the officials' approval, and that none of the opposition parties are allowed to consolidate support at the expense of the government. Recognizing the strategic value of the juntas, government officials invariably participate either directly or indirectly in the formation of new juntas to ensure that junta presidents and their lieutenants will regulate barrio politics in a way consistent with the interest of the governing party. As a consequence, most juntas represent better the interests of the government than they do the interests of the communities which elect them.

Usually the absence of an effective and determined opposition among barrio neighbors permits the juntas to perform their regulatory functions without much assistance from the government. However, at times of severe political instability, when the governing party has felt its dominance threatened, it has given certain junta presidents enough support to allow them to exercise almost dictatorial control over their communities. Such was the case, for instance, in Caracas during the 1963 election campaign when the urban guerrilla warfare carried on by the extreme left was at its height. Since the *guerrilleros* were seeking to involve large numbers of barrio residents in their activities, it was imperative, from the governing party's point of view, to bolster as fully as possible the power of its loyal barrio leaders. For example, the junta president of Caracas' most populous barrio was given not only the personal endorsement of several high-ranking government officials, but also two well-paying jobs: one, as a construction foreman on an urban renewal project, enabled him to hand out jobs to his and his party's followers; the other, as a policeman, permitted him to take direct measures to thwart the efforts of his opponents.

The juntas have been most effective as political agents of the governing party in their respective cities when they have been members of so-called junta federations. These loosely knit organizations—most often one to a city—have been established at different times by municipal or state authorities for the ostensible purpose of acting as central clearing houses for petitions for barrio improvements. It is the job of the federation president (a non-barrio, government appointee) to study junta petitions and to match them with the available resources of the various government agencies. However, the

federations have also had important political functions. Because they are usually the most accessible channel of material
assistance for the individual juntas, and because their membership is often restricted by municipal authorities to juntas
which either support the government party or remain independent, the federations provide a fairly effective instrument
for weakening opposition parties in the barrios. In addition,
the federations give the leaders of their member juntas an
authority independent of that derived from their barrios, and
this of course makes them less vulnerable to dissension from
within.

The first such organizations were set up in 1958 as part of
the Plan de Emergencia and were called Federaciones de
Juntas Pro-Mejoras (pro-betterment) . They were dominated
by different parties in different cities, and for about two years
they were able to perform their coordinating and partisan
functions fairly well. Then they began to disintegrate. In
many cases their demise can be attributed to the fact that
member juntas, discouraged by the lack of material support
received from the government after the termination of the
Plan de Emergencia in August 1959, lost their original enthusiasm.[9] In several of the central cities, juntas had been
closely associated with the Communist Party, and when its
power diminished they were unable to carry on. In other
areas the Pro-Mejoras system became the tool of profit-seeking
opportunists and was therefore discredited. In recent years,
attempts have been made to revive some of the inactive federations under different leadership (in Puerto Cabello, for example) or to establish completely new organizations (most
notably in Caracas; see Chapter 7) .

As a result of these various experiences with the government, the unaligned barrio man (who is in the great majority) is very uncertain in his relationship with the authorities.
When he has to deal with a representative of the municipal
council or the governor's office, he is never sure whether he
should approach him as a government official or as a party
leader. At the same time, he does not know how he himself is
regarded. Theoretically, as a citizen he should receive the

same treatment as all his neighbors. But he usually finds that his treatment will be roughly commensurate with his support for the dominant party.*

The preceding remarks about the partisan use of official power are by no means intended to suggest that this practice is common to all officials or even to criticize the motives of those who do use power for partisan ends. A United Nations mission to Venezuela reported in 1963 that it was very impressed by the dedication and enthusiasm of the local government officials,[10] and there is ample evidence in every town and city to support this view. Moreover, as we have already indicated, the practice stems not so much from the character of the individual officials as from the nature of the party, electoral, and fiscal systems, which partly predetermine the officials' priorities. By the same token, neither do we mean to suggest that the tendency toward this practice is unique to Venezuela. It is obviously a characteristic of local government in many nations, some of which have had much longer experience with party politics. The purpose of the argument is simply to point out that, regardless of the integrity and dedication of the officials, partisan discrimination is practiced frequently, and it has a pervasive and strong effect on the political attitudes of the barrio people. This is critical because it is happening just at the time they are making their judgment of the value of the democratic, multiparty system which the political leaders are trying to develop. The implications of this will be discussed in Chapter 9.

Confronted by the ponderous authority of a government that he may think is treating him unfairly, what can the average barrio resident do to make his grievances heard and apply pressure to obtain the benefits he thinks the government should give him? In other words, how can he adjust the incompatibility between the way he thinks government should function and the way it actually does function? Within the contemporary political framework, he has re-

---

* In the terminology of Almond and Verba ([159], pp. 215 ff.), he has a very weak sense of subject competence (i.e., he tends to think that he will not receive fair and serious consideration from government officials).

course to several means that can make him feel that he is not helpless.*

The most direct method, although not the most effective, is to organize a committee to call on an official and lodge a formal complaint. However, a combination of the barrio people's diffidence before authority and their sense of tact usually transforms what began as a bitter "complaint" when discussed among barrio neighbors into an innocuous "petition" when the committee is in the presence of the appropriate official. As a petition, it is no more likely to get results than the many others with which it must compete for attention.

The barrio people can count on much better results if they apply indirect pressure by putting their grievances before the public, thereby making them a matter of general concern. For this purpose, the radio and newspaper are useful. Most cities have radio stations, and it is customary for the local manager to schedule a short daily or weekly program of barrio news. Announcements of birthdays, marriages, private parties, and other such items are most common, but also included are complaints about community problems: "The

* In proportion to the number of those who have some grievances, there are, as one might expect, relatively few who have actually sought redress from the government. Nevertheless, their knowledge that these means are available to them indicates that they feel they have some power to influence unjust government policy. This attitude seems to be confirmed by the findings of the CENDES-CIS survey. When asked, "If you felt unjustly treated by the police, what do you think you could do to stop it?" Twenty-eight per cent of the respondents said that they would try to make some direct personal appeal to the local government. Again, in the Almond and Verba terminology, this suggests that they have a sense of citizen competence which is somewhat developed at the same time that their sense of subject competence is very weak. In *The Civic Culture* Almond and Verba find this same feature strikingly apparent in the political attitudes of lower-class Mexicans, as well as of Mexicans in general. ([159], p. 219, Figure 1.) The explanation they offer is to a remarkable degree consistent with what we know about Venezuelan politics. They suggest that it is a consequence of the "revolutionary political culture of Mexico," that the Mexican Revolution helped to develop a "subjective sense of political competence, but it was not a competence based on experience." Instead, the authors describe it as "aspirational and mythic." "Furthermore," they add, "the Revolution took place in a society where the institutions of an independent, rational bureaucracy had not taken root; local bureaucracy was the tool of the traditional political powers. Nor did the Revolution change this fundamentally. Bureaucracy remained subordinate to political forces and today is still an arena of political struggle." ([159], p. 229.)

creek in Barrio La Libertad flooded last Saturday and knocked down the bridge. The poor residents of that community want to know why the Municipal Council has not come out to repair it."

Likewise almost every Venezuelan city publishes a newspaper and this generally has a short section dedicated to barrio news. At the request of barrio residents, reporters may be sent out to cover potentially interesting stories. Frequently pictures appear in the papers, perhaps showing some women and children standing beside a garbage dump or a burst water line with a caption referring to their "misery" and "despair." Such tactics proved especially effective for some angry families in Maracay who had just invaded a large tract of land when the state governor challenged the municipal authorities who had permitted the invasion, and sent out his police force to remove them. Somebody got word down to the city newspaper, which immediately ran an article about the attempted eviction. The next day the largest paper in Caracas also covered it and included a picture of the families arguing with the police. Rather than assume the image of a merciless despot depriving poverty-striken Venezuelans of their right to a tiny plot of land, the governor backed down. Today the area is a thriving barrio of about 3,000 inhabitants.*

For grievances of a more general nature which do not focus on specific, tangible problems but which are broadly related to the barrio dwellers' desire for greater and fairer attention from the government, these measures are obviously inadequate. For such grievances the most realistic means of exerting pressure is through the opposition parties. Those are the only organized groups available to the barrio man which represent a serious threat or challenge to the government because they are the only ones that compete with it for what it really needs in order to exist—votes.

---

* The Brazilian writer Jorge Amado includes in his recent novel, *Shepherds in the Night* ([95], esp. pp. 251–254), an amusing and apparently faithful account of an invasion in Salvador, Bahia, which describes an almost identical situation. Threatened by the municipal authorities, the squatters got the support of a crusading reporter and his newspaper, and together they were able, after a protracted struggle, to force the officials to allow their settlement to survive.

7

The Political Parties and Their Struggle for Barrio Dominance

Thirteen political organizations participated in the Venezuelan national elections on December 1, 1963. Of the total valid votes cast, 94 per cent [1] was captured by five of the seven parties described below. Three of the top five (AD, COPEI, and URD) had been active since 1945–1946, and the other two (FND and FDP) were founded in 1963 to nominate and then support presidential candidates for the election itself. Another pair of parties (PCV and MIR), although excluded by law from participating in the elections, has nevertheless in recent years played a significant role in national and local politics—and thus, like the major legal parties, in the dynamics of barrio affairs.*

Acción Democrática (AD). Founded in 1941 by Rómulo Betancourt, AD was the dominant force in the government between 1945 and 1948. Under its aegis, Rómulo Gallegos was elected president in 1947—the first man in the nation's history to assume that office as the result of a national election. His administration was ended in late 1948 by a military coup. For ten years under the dictatorship of Pérez Jiménez which followed, the AD party was outlawed, and many of its leaders exiled. Nevertheless, its underground organization re-

* The eight political organizations (not all were bona fide parties) which received the remaining 6 per cent of the vote represented a broad range of political views, but, with the exception of AD-OP (*see p. 99*), had virtually no barrio following.

mained strong enough so that it was able to play an active role in the Revolution of January 1958. At the end of that year its candidate, Betancourt himself, won the presidential elections with 49.2 per cent of the vote.* After a short-lived experiment with URD in a tri-party coalition which ended in 1960, AD and its junior partner COPEI governed together until the end of the constitutional five-year term, February 1964. In 1960 AD's entire youth movement split off and formed a party of its own, Movimiento de Izquierda Revolucionaria (MIR). AD suffered another loss with the defection in 1962 of a faction led by Raúl Rámos Giménez (called Acción Democrática en Oposición, or AD-OP). Nevertheless, with Raúl Leoni as its candidate, AD won the elections of 1963, but with only 32.8 per cent of the congressional vote. After much negotiating, it then formed a new coalition with URD and FND; but in 1966 FND dropped out.

Although ideologically AD can be classified as left of center, it has been compelled—mainly by its own commitment to the industrialization of the nation and by the constant and violent pressure from the extreme left—to adopt government policies that are more in the center of Venezuela's political spectrum.

In 1958 AD's electoral support came predominantly from the rural areas. At that time the absence of barrio backing for the party was most striking in the Federal District and the major cities of the central states, although during subsequent years this imbalance has been partially adjusted.

PARTIDO SOCIAL CRISTIANO (COPEI).** Founded in 1946, its leader has always been Rafael Caldera, who was its presidential candidate in 1958 when the party won 15.2 per cent of the vote. While participating in the coalition with AD, it controlled three ministries. Caldera was again the candidate in 1963, and this time COPEI moved into second place, with 20.8 per cent of the vote. Though invited, it decided against joining again in a coalition.

---

* For a brief description of the Venezuelan electoral system, see pp. 84–85.
** COPEI, as the party is generally referred to, is the abbreviated form of the party's original name which has long since been abandoned.

COPEI has a reputation of being the "best educated" party, and it points to the large number of lawyers among its members to support this image. It was originally a very conservative organization, but over the years, especially as a result of persecution under the Pérez Jiménez dictatorship, it moved to the left and now advocates a progressive program consistent with Christian Democratic reformism.

Traditionally, the bulk of COPEI's support had come from the Andean states, but since 1958 the party has been able to build up its strength nationally, particularly among middle-class women. Though it has a highly dedicated core of workers in the barrios, its appeal in that sector has not yet proved to be great.

UNIÓN REPUBLICANA DEMOCRÁTICA (URD). It was founded in 1945 by Jóvito Villalba, who has remained its leader ever since. During the Pérez Jiménez dictatorship when AD was outlawed, URD won the national elections of 1952, although the results were immediately nullified by Pérez Jiménez. With Wolfgang Larrazábal, the president of the Provisional Government, as its candidate in the 1958 election, URD got 26.8 per cent of the congressional vote, mainly because of big majorities in the principal central cities (60 per cent, for instance, in the Federal District). After leaving the coalition with AD and COPEI in 1960, URD moved into active opposition and, under pressure from its own left wing, aligned itself on many issues with the Communist party and MIR. However, during the 1963 campaign Villalba, then the presidential candidate, adopted a more independent stance. URD won 17.3 per cent of the total party votes, and subsequently joined in a new coalition with AD and FND. In 1966 it suffered an important loss when a faction led by Ugarte Pelayo split off.

The political ideology of URD has drifted about, but today it is not significantly different from AD's. The 1958 elections showed that URD was much the strongest party in the barrios, but since its dissociation from Larrazábal, who became the nucleus of a new party, FDP in 1963, barrio support for URD has diminished substantially.

FRENTE NACIONAL DEMOCRÁTICA (FND). Organized in 1963 as Independientes Pro-Frente Nacional (IPFN) to support the candidacy of Arturo Uslar Pietri, it changed its name shortly after the elections. Uslar Pietri, who was a minister from 1941 to 1945 in the Medina administration, an independent senator from 1959 to 1964, and in private life a respected historian and literary figure, appealed to the electorate principally on the basis of his reputation as a candidate with no commitments to any of the traditional parties. On most issues, he was slightly to the right of center; he was the only candidate, for instance, who advocated relaxing the restrictions on the oil companies' exploration of new reserves which had been imposed since 1959. Nevertheless, he sought support from every quarter, including the Communists. Uslar himself won 16 per cent of the presidential vote, while his party got 13 per cent of the congressional vote. The most consistent support came from the urban middle classes, though in the large cities of the central states many barrio votes were attracted as well. FND's subsequent decision to join the coalition with AD and URD was one for which Uslar Pietri was severely criticized by many of his early backers. Later, in 1966 the party withdrew from the government and joined the opposition.

FUERZA DEMOCRÁTICA POPULAR (FDP). The party was founded in 1963 by Jorge Dáger, an ex-AD and ex-MIR member, to prepare for the coming elections in support of the candidacy of Wolfgang Larrazábal, who had been the president of the Provisional Government and the URD nominee in 1958. FDP proposed a more radical program than any of the other legal parties, and Larrazábal was the only candidate to make a major issue of imperialism. His campaign was directed almost entirely to the barrios, where his association with the Plan de Emergencia had made him very popular. Approximately four-fifths of FDP's 9.9 per cent of the total vote came from metropolitan Caracas, Maracay, Valencia, and Maracaibo.

PARTIDO COMUNISTA VENEZOLANO (PCV) and MOVIMIENTO DE IZQUIERDA REVOLUCIONARIA (MIR). The Communist party, the PCV, first organized in 1931, began to play an especially significant part in Venezuela's political life during the Pérez Jiménez dictatorship, when a semi-underground group of its members, the so-called Black Communists, was able to extend its influence into the labor unions and the field of secondary and higher education.[2] The party was active in the 1958 Revolution, and later that year supported the candidacy of Larrazábal. PCV got 6.2 per cent of the party vote. It was not invited to participate in the post-1958 coalition, and in 1960 it was joined in extreme opposition by the Movimiento de Izquierda Revolucionaria, the Marxist youth movement which, under the leadership of Domingo Alberto Rangel, had just broken off from AD. Together, members of the two parties PCV and MIR, launched an anti-government campaign of rural and urban guerrilla warfare which was conducted under the name of the Fuerzas Armadas de Liberación Nacional (FALN). The government suspended their right to operate openly as political parties in 1962, and finally made them illegal the following year.

The lack of success of the extremists' guerrilla campaign led some key figures in both PCV and MIR to doubt the wisdom of their strategy. In 1965 a group which came to be known as the "soft-liners" of MIR broke away and later integrated with the newly founded PRIN party. Subsequently, in 1966, MIR dissolved altogether. Similarly, the Communist party then began to change its tack and also to sponsor non-violent policies. Limited but persistent guerrilla activities, however, are still being carried on by the FALN, which is now composed principally of the old "hard-line" *miristas*.

During the first two years following the 1958 Revolution, PCV leaders were very influential in many barrios throughout the country. Subsequently, for reasons that will be discussed later in this chapter, this strength has been depleted. Members of MIR, although more numerous, were generally much younger and, except in Caracas, did not play a significant role in barrio affairs.*

---

* Several other parties whose political stance could theoretically attract a barrio following, but which have yet to prove themselves, have been founded since the 1963 elections. The most important of these, Partido Revolucionario

Party Membership

Party politics are a constant ingredient in barrio affairs. They play a strong role in determining the way neighbors relate with one another. Close acquaintanceships among men are as likely to be based on common party affiliations as they are on the fact that they live on the same street, hail from the same region of the country, or work for the same company. Party affiliations determine not only with whom one should associate, but also with whom one should *not* associate. In consequence, most communities are split into several mutually antagonistic groups.

Concern with party politics is found in many, seemingly irrelevant, phases of daily life. For example, a man must be careful when he chooses the color he paints his rancho, lest he unwittingly label himself a supporter of a particular party.* A foreigner wearing a beard is instinctively assumed to be affiliated with one of the parties of the far left because of its association with Fidel Castro. If a public meeting is held at the home of a prominent party member, many politically unaligned persons refuse to attend simply because they are reluctant to be identified with his party.

Barrio people are so familiar with the ways of party politics that they assume any group activity is probably motivated by party interests. In fact, as we have seen earlier, one of the most difficult aspects of eliciting barrio dwellers' participation in a community project is trying to overcome their fear of being exploited by barrio leaders representing one of the contending parties.

de Integración Nacional (PRIN), was formed in July 1966 out of three minor splinter groups: Raul Rámos Giménez's Partido Revolucionario Nacionalista (PRN, and formerly AD-OP), Vanguardia Popular Nacionalista (VPN), and the "soft-liners" of MIR. Two other parties—Movimiento Demócrata Independiente and Alianza Popular Independiente—were formed in the spring of 1966 out of groups that splintered off from URD and FND, respectively.

* To facilitate voting by illiterates, each party has its own officially designated color, or color schemes. For example, AD's is black (having changed from white in 1963 when the Supreme Electoral Council had to settle a dispute between AD and AD-OP as to which faction could retain the party's traditional color); COPEI's is green; and FDP's is silver and blue.

Only a relatively small proportion of barrio residents are actually members of any party.* However, since it is around those few that community politics usually revolve, their importance is considerably greater than their numbers suggest. In considering reasons why barrio men or women join parties, it is important to make a distinction between those parties that share political power on the municipal and state levels and those that do not. Most persons who join a local governing party do so because they hope to obtain specific benefits. Of these, the most consistently appealing is the employment which patronage offers. Another is preferential treatment from junta leaders and party officials with respect to living conditions in the barrios. This might include the opportunity to select the best plots of land at a new invasion site, the location of the scarce public water spigots near the homes of party members, or free construction materials from a government depository. Finally, prestige can be a very satisfying reward for joining a governing party, especially to persons of the aspiring class who already have steady jobs and therefore less need to rely on the government for economic advancement. By identifying themselves closely with the party in power, they acquire a sense of importance not otherwise possible. Sometimes this sense is substantiated by firm backing from partisan-oriented officials, but more often it is derived merely from being a part of an elite, "in" group.

Those who join an opposition party also hope to gain access to specific benefits. To a small extent they seek immediate compensation for their allegiance, but since the party they choose lacks the advantages of government power, such compensation is usually limited to part-time work as an organizer or recruiter for the party itself. More often they expect to be compensated at some future time; they gamble on the possibility that today's opposition party will be tomorrow's governing party. One way for this change to come about is, of course, for the opposition party to win the next

* As we indicated earlier, hard data on party membership at the barrio level are not available. However, a rough estimate based on conversations with various barrio leaders is that between 15 and 25 per cent of adult males and females in a given barrio are members of some political party.

elections—either at the national level, which would give it control of the state government; or at the municipal level, which would give it control of the city government. Such a gamble paid off, for example, for the persons in Puerto Cabello who joined Uslar Pietri's party (FND) when it was just being formed in 1963, and, after the elections, found themselves the beneficiaries of a municipal council dominated by FND members. Another way an opposition party can come to share official power is to be invited to participate in a coalition government. This method proved very rewarding for numerous barrio members of URD, for instance, who, after loyally supporting their party throughout the three lean years of the AD-COPEI administration, suddenly discovered in 1964 their luck had changed when URD accepted President Leoni's bid to join a new coalition with AD, and when, as a consequence, the party received the governorships of several states.

Additionally—and the situation in Venezuela is no exception—any opposition party tends to be more flexible and offer greater opportunities within its organization for quick advancement to new recruits than the government parties. Since they do not share in official political power, the old-guard members do not have so many interests and privileges to protect and can afford therefore to be more receptive to young "upstarts." [3]

Except for young people, party allegiance motivated by a belief in party principles is not common—certainly not so common as the intensity of the inter-party antagonism suggests. Nevertheless, such intense beliefs have attracted some members to certain parties, particularly the Communist party and its former ally, Movimiento de Izquierda Revolucionaria. For a barrio man who is vehemently and sincerely opposed to the current government, no other parties have been able to offer such a clear-cut course for active opposition —although, COPEI's dedication to Christian Democratic reformism draws a number of conscientious Catholics into its fold.

As to why so many barrio residents do not join any party,

the main reason seems to be a sense of political incompetence. People tend to assume that only the clever persons known as *políticos,* who have an inside track to those in power, are able to take advantage of party membership. Realizing that the available benefits are of very limited supply, they are reluctant to exert themselves without some assurance that the effort will be worth their while. Not infrequently such wariness is a result of previous disappointments; persons have joined parties with high expectations only to find themselves later *"engañado,"* or "deceived." Many barrio men and women also lack personal ambition and have a weak sense of urgency concerning the improvement of their own conditions. Some independents see an advantage in straddling the fence, never formally committing themselves to any one organization but remaining a friend of them all. Others adamantly dislike the whole flavor of politics and believe that only opportunists and crooks get involved in them. Finally, there are those who are confident that they can prosper on their own and do not want to be disturbed by associating with anybody but their families and close acquaintances.

Youth (ages fifteen to twenty-three) deserves special mention because of a marked tendency to shy away from the established parties even though party affiliation is possible long before voting age. Young people are not yet so concerned with the problem of getting employment, and those with any inclination toward politics are much more interested in action and a cause than in prestige or influence over their contemporaries. The most appealing parties for barrio youth, therefore, have been MIR (prior to its dissolution in 1966), the Communist Youth Movement, and FND, the new "independent" organization of Uslar Pietri. For a period during the Betancourt administration URD, although one of the traditional parties, attracted considerable support from this age group—mainly, however, because of its "untraditional" militant left wing and its identification with Larrazábal. The idealism of COPEI, although a powerful force among university students, is apparently a bit too sophisticated for most barrio people of the same age. Acción Democrática is struggling hard, especially since the 1963 elections, to rebuild its youth wing—in Caracas, for instance, it has organized special sports programs for this purpose—but it still presents a generally uninspiring image to the young.

The range of duties and responsibilities of party membership is wide, and it varies with the cohesiveness of parties' organizations and the strength of their ideologies. Many barrio members contribute nothing more than their votes and their signature on party lists, except during the election campaigns. Then, mobilized by party workers, they attend the large, open-air rallies and cheer the speeches of their candidates, display party signs on their ranchos, and hang propaganda on lamp posts and municipal buildings. Members of COPEI, AD, and now FND are occasionally obliged by the parties' hierarchies to work on community projects and contribute money for special party activities. Members of the two parties of the extreme left, PCV and, until recently, MIR, are much more closely directed and have been called on to join in demonstrations, or, in the past, to participate in their terrorist campaign.

Party Politics

In order to analyze partisan politics in the barrios, it is necessary to recognize that the partisan contention in these communities derives its energy from the interaction of the various party organizations on the municipal and state levels. It is the money, time, and effort that party officials spend on increasing membership and developing voter strength in their respective cities that determines the intensity of the struggle in the barrios and the number of parties which are involved in it.

The extent to which barrio politics is a derivative of municipal and state politics can be seen in the close correspondence in the degree of conflict or cooperation among parties on the two levels. Valencia's experience during the Betancourt administration offers a particularly clear illustration. The three parties which at that time shared seats on the Municipal Council—AD, URD, and COPEI—were able to work out a comfortable modus vivendi among themselves that contributed substantially to the Council's ability to promote so effectively the development of its industrial zone. Similarly, their relations with each other on the barrio level were uncharacteristically compatible. For example, Valencia had one of the few barrios in Venezuela whose affairs were actively and productively managed by a multi-party junta.

Yet regardless of such parallels in inter-party relationships between the barrio and the municipal levels, there is seldom a similar parallel on the national level. While AD and COPEI worked closely together in the coalition government of 1959–1963, their barrio members were bitter enemies in many areas. Caracas, the new junta federation, which had counted heavily on a partnership arrangement between the two parties when it was founded in 1962, suffered a serious setback the following year when COPEI publicly denounced the federation as a tool of AD power and instructed its members to withdraw their support. Similarly, the traditional rivalry between URD and AD still prevails in most communities today, despite the supposedly amiable relationship among their leaders in the Leoni cabinet.

Within the barrios, the number of contending parties varies from city to city. In a few cities, the power of a single party is so well established that party membership is notably uniform among barrio dwellers. In most, however, two or three parties are significantly represented in almost every barrio. In Caracas, strong coteries of all the major political groupings are active.

It was suggested earlier that the particular party within a community that enjoys the support of the government agencies is usually dominant. However, this simple cause-and-effect relationship is complicated by the fact that there are two separate sources of political power within each city—emanating, on the one hand, from the municipal council president, and, on the other, from the state governor—which do not necessarily represent the same allegiances. A municipality where the majority of votes go to a party in opposition to the party of the President of the Republic will be governed by a municipal council president of one party (the party that won the district election) and a governor of another (the President's own, since he appoints the governor). Both parties will therefore have authority and spheres of influence. Caracas, Maracay, and Puerto Cabello are three of the cities which have been characterized by this duality in recent years.* On the other hand, one-party control of both municipal and state offices has been an important feature of politics in Maracaibo, Ciudad Guayana, and Puerto La Cruz.

Where duality exists, political contention manifests itself in the ambivalent nature of barrio politics as leaders appeal to two different authorities, depending on their particular allegiances and needs. Maracay, in the state of Aragua, offers a good example. During both recent Acción Democrática administrations, the city government has been in the hands of an opposition party: first URD, later FDP. Throughout most of this period, Aragua state has had AD governors. Consequently, some barrios have been dominated by one party, some by another. Often communities have had two juntas, each claiming to be the official representative body. There has also been constant conflict over the formation of new barrios by invasion ** because the governors have been committed to a policy of strict control while the municipal council presidents have been extremely lenient.

This might seem to indicate that the strengths of the two parties would be roughly balanced were the state and city governments in different hands. In fact, however, the scales are weighted heavily in favor of the governor. Being directly linked to the various federal ministries, agencies, and institutes whose local representatives he is empowered to appoint, the governor is far better able to extend patronage than the municipal council president. In the interior, his contacts

---

* Division of government powers also results when local offices are held by two different parties as the consequence of a coalition arrangement. For a period, barrio affairs in Cabimas, for instance, mirrored the fact that the president of the junta federation was AD and the police chief, the *prefecto,* FND.

** For an interesting account of the struggle between two juntas representing different parties for the control of a barrio recently settled in Ciudad Bolívar, see *El Nacional,* November 8, 1965, p. d-4.

with the Ministry of Public Works and the National Institute of Sanitary Works (INOS) have been particularly useful for this purpose; in Caracas, he has influence with the Centro Simón Bolívar, C.A., the government-owned construction company that is handling the urban renewal program, which is an effective source of patronage. Because of these connections, the governor also has greater access to materials and equipment, and is therefore better able to support politically sympathetic barrio leaders by granting their petitions. In addition, the prefecto, whom he appoints, has proved very effective in strengthening the governor's hand in several cities of the interior. The prefecto's influence is derived, however, not so much from his ability to exert repressive control over local politics as from the prestige of his office and from his own political maneuvering.

The importance for barrio politics of the contention between municipal and state governments when the two are controlled by rival parties will become clearer when we examine the role of Acción Democrática. By virtue of its electoral victories in 1958 and 1963, AD has been in a unique position to influence barrio development. Its efforts to do this, successful or unsuccessful, have shaped the character of barrio politics to a great extent. In fact, the activities of the other major parties can only be properly assessed if seen in relation to those of AD.

ACCIÓN DEMOCRÁTICA

Acción Democrática's role in barrio politics since 1959 has been a response to the critical fact that at that time the party received most of its electoral support from the campesinos and that its influence among the urban lower class was generally very weak. When Betancourt assumed the presidency, he and his party's other leaders were acutely aware that if they were to sustain a democratically constituted administration through a full term in office for the first time in Venezuelan history, and then to hold elections that would determine its successor, one of their major tasks would have to be the extension of their influence over the political life of the barrios. The barrios were at once more densely populated and—as we shall discuss in Part III—more susceptible to partisan influences, and better able to be mobilized for mass action than any other sector of society; and if the AD administration failed to cope adequately with them, the extreme leftist parties would probably succeed in dominating barrio politics, and thus be able to cause enough political instability to justify military seizure of the government. Moreover, even if the immediate problem of political instability could be eliminated, the rapid numerical growth of rancho dwellers relative to other sectors of society made it imperative that AD strengthen substantially its very precarious electoral position. The outlines of AD's task in this area, then, were clear: it had to act as a political stabilizer at the same time that it served as an agent for social and economic progress.

The party approached the problem from three different angles. The three approaches are interrelated, but in order to assess the impact of each, we must discuss them separately.

First, AD sought to strengthen its position by increasing the number of its barrio members. Without a large rank-and-file support, the party would have been almost powerless to extend the federal government's development programs into this sector. Yet in early 1959, when Betancourt came to power, AD's membership in the barrios, relative to that of the other parties, was at an all-time low. Partly responsible for this state of affairs was the severe persecution the party had suffered at the hands of Pérez Jiménez. It had been the primary target of the dictator's repression, and most of its older and experienced leaders were either exiled, jailed, or murdered. However, as bad as it was, AD's condition at the time of the Revolution was not so much worse than that of the other parties. That it did not recuperate more successfully was the result of another, more critical factor that came into play in 1958 and can best be illustrated by what happened in Caracas.*

The leaders who were in charge of Acción Democrática's organization, recruitment, and election campaign in 1958

* The following account is based on an analysis of AD's difficulties in Caracas by Gabriel Moro [31].

were for the most part the young members who had remained in Venezuela during the dictatorship and had been
active in the underground movement; many of them later
would leave the party and form the radical Movimiento de
Izquierda Revolucionaria. They resented having to relin-
quish the party reins to the "old guard" leaders who were
just returning from exile and, rather than work enthusiastically for the old party organization, they supported, either
actively or by default, AD's principal rivals, URD and PCV.
Even the Plan de Emergencia was administered by one of
these dissident AD leaders who, rather than designate AD
partisans or, at least, independents, to distribute the vast
stock of favors that the Plan made available, appointed men
who, as one balanced account puts it, were "frequently Communists, or anti-Betancourt *adecos,* when they were not pro-
Larrazalistas." [4] With such unreliable support from many of
its principal organizers, AD was at a great disadvantage from
the beginning, and by the time of the elections in December
1958, it could count on only 8,000 members in the entire
capital.[5] It was little wonder then that the party placed
fourth in the balloting in the Federal District, receiving less
than 15 per cent of the votes cast.

Following the elections, AD leaders launched a nationwide
campaign of reorganization and recruitment in the barrios.
Around the core of faithful members then available, they
systematically built up a vast network of formal membership
groups. Known as *comités de barrios,* these groups have become the base units of the party organization in the urban
areas, and their headquarters are now found in virtually
every barrio in the country. Members meet once a week and
discuss, besides matters of purely party interest such as individual duties, dues, and so forth, the affairs and problems of
their respective barrios. As stated in the party's manual, one
of their principal functions is to recruit new members from
among friends and neighbors.[6]

Important as the comités have been for organizing and
consolidating the rank and file of Acción Democrática, it is
unlikely that they have been the principal key to the actual

recruitment process. As we have seen already, a barrio man generally has to have some positive evidence that he will actually benefit from the association before becoming a member of a particular political party. Such evidence must usually come from the party's higher echelons. In the case of AD, the most effective persuasion was, of course, patronage. By offering men employment or opportunities to play influential roles within their communities, the party was able to entice large numbers into its fold. In August 1959, the party claimed a national membership of 795,061.[7] By July 1962, when it took its next census, in spite of having lost its entire youth movement when MIR split off and another faction when AD-OP joined the opposition, the total membership had risen to 903,282. This increase of 14 per cent is especially impressive when we note that it was achieved mainly in the cities, as revealed by the fact that in the five most urbanized states,* AD membership increased by an average 57 per cent. In Caracas alone, the total number of members rose to more than 40,000 in early 1963 (from 8,000 in late 1958).[8] In the state of Zulia, with well over half its population in the two cities of Maracaibo and Cabimas where both the state and municipal governments were controlled by AD, membership nearly doubled in the period between the two censuses, from 60,000 to 117,000. Since the advantages of membership are really only relevant to the needs of the lower classes, we can assume that almost all the increase came from that sector; and in the urban areas this meant that the greatest portion came from the barrios.**

* These are the five states—the Federal District, Zulia, Miranda, Carabobo, and Aragua—which had the highest proportion of persons living in urban areas, according to the 1961 census. Figures are derived from *Anuario Estadístico de Venezuela, 1957–1963*. ([89], Cuadros 113 and 135.)

** It is interesting to note that in seven states, all of which were predominantly rural, AD membership actually decreased from 1959 to 1962. This fact points to one or both of two possibilities: that the success of the recruitment campaign was limited for the most part to the urban areas, and/or that the increase in urban members was due at least to some extent to the migration from the countryside to the cities of campesinos with AD affiliations. If the latter were true, however, it seems unlikely that the flow of these particular campesinos would have been strong or consistent enough to invalidate the conclusions drawn above.

As the 1963 elections drew near, AD's emphasis shifted from the recruitment of new members to consolidation of its hold over old ones; it became clear that if the party could keep all its membership under its wing until election time in December, it would be virtually assured of an electoral victory. It is likely, too, the party decided it had reached something like a saturation point, beyond which party and government facilities could not absorb more members without the danger of disappointing their hopes and thereby increasing rather than decreasing the number of opposition votes. During this period, one considered oneself either "in" or "out" with respect to AD; there were few so-called *simpatizantes,* nonmembers who voted with that party. As we shall see, this fact was reflected in the results of the elections.

As Betancourt's administration secured its position and the dominance of his party became widely recognized, members of this "in" group began to nurture an image of themselves as guardians of the national government. They believed, and the AD officials confirmed, that they had heavy responsibilities on the local level to maintain the sort of order that the President needed to succeed with his program for Venezuela's development. Their sense of eliteness gave rise to a clublike fraternalism reflected, for instance, in their use of the special greeting *"compañero!";* in their defensiveness; and in their wariness of the participation of non-members in community projects.

The second approach Acción Democrática used to attack the problem of its weakness in the barrios was to seek control over organized community leadership by dominating the juntas and molding them into instruments of its governing policies. At the beginning of Betancourt's administration, leadership in the great majority of barrios in most major cities was in the hands of non-AD members, mostly Communists and *urdistas,* a situation resulting from heavy material support to the Juntas Pro-Mejoras by officials antagonistic to AD.

Confronted with this predicament, the AD-dominated Government would have liked, of course, to move immediately to open up barrio politics and break the opposition's virtual monopoly. However, several obstacles stood in its way. On the barrio level, the obvious handicap was the very weak condition of AD membership. AD was also in a disadvantageous position on the municipal and state level. The municipal councils would have been the most natural and logical seat of authority through which to channel its efforts, but in 1959 only a handful were firmly controlled by AD party members. Likewise, on the state level its hands were tied at first because of the many anti-AD elements which still shared governing powers. URD, as part of the coalition arrangement, held several of the key governorships. The Communists were still influential in a number of social organizations, and their status was protected by their friendly relations with URD. Moreover, there was still a powerful group of anti-Betancourt, future mirista leaders in the AD party.

As it turned out, AD's first major attempt to undermine the opposition's control of juntas—terminating the Plan de Emergencia in August 1959—could be easily justified on purely economic and social grounds. The Plan was placing an enormous, unproductive burden on the Treasury; Betancourt himself estimated that in less than a year and a half it had cost the country 600 million bolivares.[9] Nevertheless, cutting the lifeline of many of the juntas which had depended upon that source of assistance had a decisive political impact of which AD was certainly aware. As it had undoubtedly expected, the action caused a strong reaction among barrio dwellers, which led to riots and street demonstrations in Caracas. But AD and the government were convinced that allowing the increasingly antagonistic opposition parties to exploit the Plan, as a way of further consolidating their control over barrio politics, represented a risk as great, if not greater, to national stability.

Following the termination of the Plan, the juntas associated with the opposition parties found it very difficult to get government assistance. When they went to the state and federal agencies petitioning for communal facilities, they got nothing but tales of hard times and meager government budgets. Since the opposition junta leaders had promoted themselves, among their barrio neighbors, as agents for community improvement and such improvements depended almost entirely on government assistance no longer forthcoming, their influence over their communities steadily weakened.

The effect of this "embargo" tactic would not have been so decisive if the municipal governments controlled by the opposition had countered the AD strategy with programs of their own to help sustain the prestige of sympathetic juntas. Yet, after the Communist party's influence in government circles began to wane, URD demonstrated a marked inability to cope with the problem. Lack of finances was doubtless partially responsible, but observation of several cities dominated by URD indicates that the failure can be more accurately attributed to official incompetence. In Puerto Cabello, for example, URD officials showed little interest in barrio affairs and threw away their chances for lasting control by allowing a formerly strong federation of juntas to be run by an old man who claimed to be a Communist, but who had no appreciable support from any party. Consequently, when AD finally shifted to the offensive and moved to extend its authority over Puerto Cabello barrios through the local prefecto, it encountered almost no resistance.

The political emasculation of unsympathetic juntas was not the end goal of the AD strategy. Rather, as a vacuum was created by the demise of the old leadership, the party stepped in to establish its own foothold. In a few cities, the task was not difficult. In Valencia, for example, aggressive party leaders had managed to capture control of the federation of Juntas Pro-Mejoras as early as 1958, and, although the individual juntas were not all in AD hands, the party's dominance was firmly enough established that it was never seriously threatened by the opposition. However, in most towns and cities AD did not enjoy this advantage, and the job of promoting its interests was demanding—particularly in Caracas, where, as we shall see, AD has expended more money and effort for this purpose than in any other city.

In 1958 Acción Democrática received less than 15 per cent

of the votes in the Federal District (which includes most of metropolitan Caracas) and ran fourth, behind URD, PCV, and COPEI. In 1959 Caracas' Municipal Council, junta federation and the individal juntas were all dominated by representatives or friends of URD and PCV. After the cessation of the Plan de Emergencia, whose benefits were most heavily distributed in Caracas, AD officials used the same "embargo" tactic described above and allowed the juntas to wither away. A two-year period of party inactivity followed; then in the spring of 1962, again working through the governor's office, AD set about forming a new federation of juntas known as the Movimiento Pro-Desarrollo de la Comunidad. Like all such organizations, the Movimiento called itself non-partisan and said it sought the support of all persons who were interested in the welfare of their communities.[10] However, very little was actually done to disguise its close affiliation with AD.[11] The man appointed by the governor to be president of the Movimiento was well known in barrio circles as a militant adeco of long standing. In an interview with U.S. Embassy representatives, he himself stated that the Movimiento was designed to "isolate and eliminate leftist groups."

As would have been expected, therefore, when in 1962 elections were held to select junta members in several key Caracas barrios, the opposition—aware that only government-approved juntas could expect membership and benefits from the Movimiento—boycotted those elections. Consequently, the resulting juntas were organized around three members of AD, three members of COPEI (the coalition partner at the time), and one Independent. A number of juntas so composed were formed in barrios in western Caracas until COPEI announced its withdrawal from the federation. Subsequently the Movimiento's policies have relaxed somewhat. Influenced by some prominent failures of staunchly AD-controlled juntas and the success of several popularly-based ones, its president has come to accept participation in the Movimiento by independent groups.

Acción Democrática also used a third approach in its attempt to improve its position in the barrios. Toward the end of the third year of Betancourt's administration (early in 1962), it began openly to sponsor urban community development. In theory, at least, this was a more subtle approach than AD had tried before, using indirect methods to obtain what it was hoped would be long-term benefits for the party.

Community development methods were already familiar to Venezuela at that time. Since 1960 the national government had strongly supported a vigorous and extensive program organized by the División de Desarrollo de la Comunidad of Cordiplan (Oficina Central de Coordinación y Planificación) and known as the National Program of Community Development. A pioneer in its field in Latin America, the program was soon to receive wide international acclaim for its imaginative use of national and local resources to promote self-help community projects.[12] It was an "integrative" type of program [13] which relied heavily on coordination among government agencies to provide the material and technical assistance needed for community improvement projects.

By February 1962, the program had been initiated in eight states.[14] However, it had confined itself almost entirely to the rural areas and a few medium-sized cities of the interior.* The main reason why it had not yet been extended into the major urban areas was probably indicated by the program director who, late in 1961, advised the workers of a similar private organization just beginning its operations, not to work in Caracas because nothing effective could be done there in the face of vehement anti-government sentiment.[15] She herself had experimented in two Caracas barrios, but had found the leftist control of community politics too great an obstacle to overcome, and finally had decided to abandon them.**

---

* For a full description of the most successful project in one of the medium-sized cities of the interior, see Carola Ravell [39]. Other such projects were in San Carlos, San Félix, Cumaná, and San Cristóbal.

** Prior to 1962 Banco Obrero, the lower-class housing agency, had also sponsored some community development activities in Caracas, but only in the superbloques. In March 1960 it began a program in the group of superbloques known as Simón Rodríguez, whose residents were socially and economically among the most advanced of superbloque inhabitants. The program involved primarily mothers and children and met with considerable

Although the rural-oriented program was firmly backed by AD and was most successful in the areas where that party was dominant, it was generally not identified with the party. The director herself was not a member of AD and, according to sources close to her, she withstood continual pressure from the party in order to keep her program politically independent. There is no doubt, however, that AD's experience with community development in the rural areas did much to encourage the party to promote similar activities in the barrios as it came to recognize the benefits that could accrue to the party, as well as to the communities themselves. Were its initiative to be successful, went the party reasoning, AD members would show the rancho dwellers that by working hand in hand with the government they had the ability to solve their most urgent problems and to make the barrios a better place in which to live. As a result, a spirit of progress, self-improvement and mutual trust would permeate the poorer communities. By virtue of being the principal government party, AD would be recognized as an agent for development, and its prestige would grow accordingly. Further, by taking this initiative, the party would thwart the efforts of its rivals, especially those of the extreme left, to rally support and undermine political stability.

As the word passed through the party echelons during the early months of 1962, municipal and barrio leaders began talking of the concepts of *desarrollo comunal:* * Stagnancy should no longer be accepted as the natural condition of the barrios, and barrio leaders should not be content just to petition the government offices and wait for the desired improvements to be provided. Instead, city officials and barrio residents alike should take up the banner of desarrollo comunal and work together for the welfare of the poor communities:

success. Somewhat later a similar effort was made in another group, 23 de enero, where the socio-economic level of the residents was closer to that of the barrios. Its effectiveness there was much more limited, due mainly to severe problems of a political nature that discouraged community participation. [6]

* In order to avoid confusion with the predominantly rural National Program of Community Development, the term *desarrollo comunal* will be used to refer to AD-sponsored activities in urban areas.

the officials by offering encouragement and the material and technical assistance required, the barrio members by awakening an interest in community progress and encouraging their neighbors to cooperate with one another. Desarrollo comunal should be open to all those who were interested in bettering their condition; there should be no partisan discrimination. Subsequently, phrases such as "the community must participate in its own progress," "the government supplies the materials, the community the labor," "desarrollo comunal is nonpartisan," and "in union there is strength" became so familiar that party leaders parroted them whenever the subject was mentioned.

However, the AD national headquarters did not follow through with systematic direction but instead left implementation of the theory entirely up to the local administrations. Consequently, in each city the activities were managed by different officials and organizations, depending upon the branch or branches of government that AD controlled and upon the personality of the individual officials. In Puerto Cabello the prefecto was the chief AD agent for desarrollo comunal. In Maracay the party channeled its efforts through the same office, ORDEC,* that had been set up to direct the rural community program in Aragua state. In the Federal District, a completely new federation of juntas was formed to stimulate community activities, and its president was the chief coordinator. In Maracaibo the Municipal Council and the Zulia branch of ORDEC were the principal promoters of the new idea. In Valencia, the old federation of Juntas Pro-Mejoras, linked closely with the party since its foundation, assumed this role.

From the beginning AD's effectiveness as a community-action promoter was severely handicapped, not only by the political obstacles it faced, but even more decisively by the

---

* Each state in which the National Program of Community Development operated had an ORDEC (Oficina Regional de Desarrollo Comunal) office, which was supposed to coordinate the activities throughout the state. The heads of each were appointed by the governor, and in some of the state capitals where these men were loyal adecos they helped to promote the party's barrio efforts.

party's own behavior. In the first place, before AD started talking up the idea of desarrollo comunal, it had not made prior arrangements to ensure that the local governments would be any better equipped financially than they had been to cope with projects promoted by their barrio leaders. Only in the Federal District were extra funds set aside. This may seem surprising in view of the fact that the AD initiative coincided almost exactly with the creation of a financing institution, the Foundation for Community Development and Municipal Improvement (COMUN).[16] COMUN was set up on the basis of a $30,000,000 loan from the Agency for International Development and matching funds from the Venezuelan Government. While its primary emphasis was to be on urban-renewal programs, it had set aside a special Fund for Community Development from which grants of up to 5,000 bolivars could be made to individual community projects, including, theoretically, those from the barrios. However, mainly because there was a long delay while the AID loan was getting cleared, the funds were not available until 1963. But even then, for reasons that were less apparent, the grants were hardly utilized at all by the municipal governments in the interior, either for barrio or other local projects.

The lack of government support, of course, had a very detrimental effect on those leaders, admittedly few, who had taken the trouble to arouse their neighbors and had counted on government backing of certain projects. One such man in Ciudad Guayana, an AD member, had for several months been grooming his community for the day when the local government would come through with its promise to supply pipe for a water system. The neighbors intended to install it themselves. He called numerous meetings; attendance was high, and so was his prestige. After much waiting, hope began rapidly fading, and with it the political career of one of the most progressive and potentially effective leaders in the city.

AD has also failed to make sure that the local officials could offer the personal guidance needed to back up the community leaders. None of them received training in how to translate the vague theories into actual practice. As a consequence, there was a good deal of talk about the ideas of desarrollo comunal, but few community projects were attempted and fewer still completed.

Finally, the greatest handicap under which desarrollo comunal had to labor was its public identification with the political interests of Acción Democrática. The importance of this stigma can best be appreciated when one considers the case of the Federal District, whose government was the only one both financially and operationally prepared to handle a significant response from its barrio leaders.

One of the incentives that led the governor's office to establish the new junta federation, the Movimiento Pro-Desarrollo de la Comunidad mentioned previously, had been the assurance of sufficient financial and material assistance to support an active organization. In the first place, it received funds indirectly (through the Comité de Remodelación) from COMUN. According to information made available to the U.S. Embassy by the Movimiento's president, it got 600,000 bolívares from this source during 1963; other reliable accounts indicate that this was about the average amount it continued to receive during the subsequent three years. Additionally, because of its close contacts with COMUN, it was in an especially good position to channel grants from the Fund for Community Development into its barrio projects.[17] Finally, because of its close link with the Centro Simón Bolívar, C.A., the publicly-owned construction company contracted to handle the barrio renewal programs, and with the other official agencies similarly involved, the Movimiento was also able to count on considerably more material assistance than junta federations outside the Federal District.

Structurally, the Movimiento was also very well equipped to sponor desarrollo comunal. As it was set up, the individual juntas, after consulting the people of their communities, were to relay their petitions for assistance to one of the ten zone offices (*jefatura de la parróquia*) which, in turn, would report them to the Movimiento's president. In case of urgent need, there was a provision allowing the juntas to bypass the intermediate step and communicate directly with the president.[18] He then would function as coordinator, securing the necessary assistance and making it available to the petitioning juntas. Afterwards, it would be the juntas' responsibility to see the projects through.

Yet the Movimiento has not been notably more successful in encouraging desarrollo communal than efforts in other cities without the Movimiento's apparent advantages. The number of projects in which barrio residents of the Federal District have played a major role is still quite small. Furthermore, it has been reported that in at least a few seemingly successful cases of neighborhood participation in such projects the incentive has been money, paid to barrio leaders and residents either directly or indirectly by the Movimiento.

The same problems leading to the relative failure of desarrollo comunal in the Federal District—principally its identification with Acción Democrática—have plagued the program in almost every city where it has been practiced. Invariably, the officials mainly involved in promotion of the communal activities—whether they represent the municipal councils, Oficina Regional de Desarrollo Comunal (ORDEC), the *prefecturas,* the federations, or whatever—have been known throughout the barrios as staunch AD supporters. Seldom has the party made significant efforts to disguise this connection by putting unaligned officials in these posts. As for the barrios themselves, the AD comités have usually been indistinguishable except by name from the Juntas Pro-Desarrollo de la Comunidad or the Juntas Pro-Mejoras. In some communities, they have not even bothered to meet in separate houses. Leaders have been known to cut junta meetings short so that they could attend their comité sessions.

For those who were not already friends of the party, this close identification of community concerns with one exclusive group has been offensive. As a consequence, politically unaligned barrio dwellers have been exceedingly reluctant to participate in activities suspected of being promoted to enhance the position of AD, even when it was realized that non-AD members would have benefitted also.

If one were to assess the overall effect of the AD strategy to guide the political role of the barrio dwellers and to build up the party's strength in that sector, probably the most useful yardstick would be the national elections of 1963, as the most clear-cut demonstration available of the barrio people's attitudes.

That the elections were held on schedule in December 1963 and that Betancourt was able to remain in office until completion of his term the following February are in themselves major accomplishments to AD's credit. It is obvious that the party's measures had greatly undermined the influence of the extreme left in the barrios and that fact, in turn, was largely the reason the barrios did not play a more aggressive role during the five years between 1958 and 1963.

There was, furthermore, the very encouraging fact that attendance at the elections was high: 92 per cent * of the registered voters cast their ballots on December 1. This high percentage represented a firm repudiation by the electorate of the extreme left's methods of expressing political dissatisfaction, since the two illegalized parties—the Communist PCV and the Movimiento de Izquierda Revolucionaria—had called for a general boycott of the elections to demonstrate popular rejection of the Betancourt regime.** This repudiation was especially satisfying to AD, which had reason to fear that its own efforts might have forced significant numbers of voters into the extremist camp.

Beyond these considerations, however, the results of the elections should have given AD cause to be unhappy with the outcome of its barrio strategy. In every state in the nation the party's relative share of the votes decreased, in some by as much as 20 to 30 per cent. Moreover, in every state except the Federal District and Amazonas, AD received fewer total votes than it had in 1958. But more pertinent to this study is the fact that only 32,000 more persons in the entire nation

* Based on the official registration figure of 3,369,986 and a total presidential vote of 3,107,563.

** It was, of course, possible that the 8 per cent who were registered but did not vote represented those who supported the boycott. However, in view of the prodding by the government and the parties that was required to get Venezuelans to register themselves (the regular 60-day period had to be extended twice, for two weeks each time, until approximately 94 per cent of the estimated eligible voters were registered), it is much more likely that their absence from the polls reflected their general lack of interest rather than their pro-extremist sentiment.

voted for AD than the party had claimed as members.* Of the five most urbanized states, Carabobo and Aragua fared the worst, with no surplus of votes over members at all. In Zulia, the total number of votes received was 8 per cent above membership, and in Miranda it was 16 per cent. The only one which registered a notable difference was the Federal District, where there were 91 per cent more votes than members. But even in this case the results must have been very disappointing to AD party leaders, who had high expectations that for every member there would be several non-member votes. In fact, Gabriel Moro was probably expressing the opinion of these leaders when he predicted a few months before the elections that one could multiply the number of AD members by four to six times and approximate the number of votes the party would receive.[19]

The almost universal rejection of Acción Democrática by non-members in every sector of society is obviously of great importance to the party. In light of our previous observations two main reasons seem to explain this response in the barrios.**

Barrio people were unimpressed by the government's progress toward improving their conditions. They had counted on being provided with the benefits of urban life, but during the five years prior to the election, they did not see much change in their status. Their general disappointment was best illustrated by the situation in Ciudad Guayana, whose industrial boom has been billed as one of the major achievements of the AD administration. Many families migrated to the area in search of promised employment, but when they got there and settled in the barrios, they found

* Although this figure is based on a census of the previous year, we can assume that it gives us a fairly accurate indication of the number of "independents" who voted for AD. The probability that the total membership continued to increase during the months remaining in 1962 and 1963 after the census more than offsets the probability that some members defected from the party and that not all members bothered to go to the polls.

** In his election analysis, Martz ([72], p. 41) refers in passing to the voting trend in the barrios, saying "although city totals are imprecise, there was general agreement that many workers' sections in Maracaibo, Valencia, Maracay, and Barquisimeto turned away from Acción Democrática."

that the jobs either had not yet been created, or were not for the unskilled. As would have been expected their displeasure was expressed at the polls in 1963, and as a consequence Acción Democrática lost a substantial number of votes as well as its control of the Municipal Council. This typical reaction by barrio voters to the first AD administration appears to have reflected their recognition and annoyance that the party had been concerned with other aspects of Venezuela's development in addition to barrio welfare. Several of the contending parties had led the barrio voters to believe that, given the opportunity to run the government, they would devote almost undivided attention to eradicating barrio problems, whereas the barrio people knew from experience that this was not the case with AD.

The other reason had more specifically political overtones and, therefore, was more closely associated with the aspiring-class barrio residents, who resented AD's use of power to further what they interpreted to be the party's own interests. They distrusted the motives of the officials on the one hand, and they were embittered by the special role of their AD neighbors on the other. Their experience with the privileges, the prestige and the protection of party members emphasized in their minds the rewards of political power that they were lacking.* The antagonism, which was conspicuous in every community, was so strong in barrios of the central cities, such as Maracay and Caracas, that it rendered futile any efforts to integrate the party and non-party elements.

In the light of the anti-AD sentiment that built up during the first administration, it would seem likely that a large number of the barrio electorate would have demonstrated

---

* Myron Weiner in *The Politics of Scarcity* ([192], p. 227) cites findings (from Baldev Raj Nayar's master's thesis, "Impact of Community Development Programs on Rural Voting Behavior in India," University of Chicago, 1959) that suggest an interesting parallel between the Indian and the Venezuelan experience with community development. In India's 1952 and 1957 elections the vote for the Congress party increased more in areas without community development programs than in those which had them. Weiner comments: "There are often socially disturbing consequences of a development project which turn sections of the local populace against the government."

their support of the opposition of the extreme left by not voting at the elections. In order to assess why this did not happen, it is necessary to examine the role of the two revolutionary parties, PCV and MIR.

THE EXTREME LEFT

Under the special political conditions that existed during 1958, members of both the Communist party and of the then radical wing of Acción Democrática were able to establish positions of real influence for themselves, both in official circles as well as on the barrio level. Also, as a result of the December 1958 elections, the two political groups enjoyed respectable representation in the National Congress. Relying on this strength, both the Communists and the future miristas, during the first year of the Betancourt administration sought as a general policy to make their pressure felt on national politics through legitimate channels. However, this began to change radically in 1960 when MIR broke away from the governing party and URD, as described at the beginning of this chapter, became increasingly antagonistic toward its two coalition partners. The change manifested itself most emphatically during the months of October and November of 1960 when, inspired by riots started by university students, PCV and MIR attempted unsuccessfully to provoke a popular insurrection. The government and anti-government forces thereupon prepared for a showdown. Betancourt moved to eliminate Communist and mirista influence in his administration, in the labor movement, and generally throughout the nation; the parties of the extreme left began to sponsor openly subversive action in a campaign which started slowly, then developed quickly during 1962 with the formation of the clandestine Fuerzas Armadas de Liberación Nacional (FALN), and reached its climax during the election year of 1963, affecting in varying degrees every area of the country.

Four different, although related, types of these left-extremist activities can be distinguished: 1) Rural guerrilla warfare, conducted most consistently in the northwestern state of Falcón, but flaring up also in other regions; 2) sabotage, concentrated on the property of North American companies, but affecting other foreign firms and government projects as well; 3) spectacular headline-makers, including the hijacking of a Venezuelan airliner and a government ship; the kidnapping of an internationally known Spanish soccer player and of U.S. military personnel; and the stealing of valuable art work from a Caracas museum; [20] 4) terrorism, particularly in the cities of the populous central states and the Federal District, in the form of bomb scares, threatening telephone calls, daylight machine-gun robberies, intimidation of barrio leaders, and the murder of policemen and national guardsmen. Although the fear that directly resulted from such terrorist activities was considerable, a much greater atmosphere of insecurity was caused by the extreme sensitivity of the various police forces constantly on guard against "abnormal" behavior. As the extremists undoubtedly had calculated, the anxiety of the police not infrequently resulted in the injury and death of innocent persons.[21]

The two leftist parties apparently reasoned that an all-out campaign against the government would succeed in one of two ways. First, by exposing the government's inability to maintain a stable political and economic environment, they expected to create a situation in which the military would feel compelled to intervene. Subsequently, the oppression of the military dictatorship combined with the public's recognition of the inherent instability, and hence futility, of a reformist administration, would convince Venezuelans of the relevance of revolutionary ideology and tactics. As a result, the Communists and their partners would emerge ultimately as the most powerful popular force. Or, second, by intensifying the already prevalent anti-government antagonism, they hoped to incite a general insurrection that would carry them directly into power without having to go through the preliminary phases of another military regime. The revolts in the garrisons of Carúpano and Puerto Cabello in 1962 suggest that not only did they consider this alternative realistic, but that they even counted on a certain amount of support from the armed forces.

Both tactics and propaganda of the far left parties made it clear that they considered the people of the barrios one of the keys to their success. The barrios, along with the university students, had been the sector of society which participated most actively and enthusiastically in the Revolution of 1958. The results of that year's elections indicated the barrios' overwhelming support for radicalism of the left, whether represented by Larrazábal, the PCV, or the dissident wing of AD. Moreover, it was the barrio dwellers who were suffering most from the economic depression into which the country had fallen after 1958. Consequently, leaders of the urban guerrilla campaign had high expectations of the barrio people's participation, as is revealed, for example, in *La Revolución de las Fantasias* by Domingo Alberto Rangel, the head of MIR throughout the period under discussion. Although Rangel refers specifically to their role in the overthrow of Pérez Jiménez, he makes amply clear that he still considers the "floating masses" of the barrios to have the greatest revolutionary potential of any sector of Venezuelan society.[22] To support his contention he refers to parallel observations made by Frantz Fanon in *The Wretched of the Earth*. Because of the two men's similarity in outlook, and because of Fanon's exalted status in revolutionary circles today as a leading ideologist of revolution in the "Third World," it is relevant to quote a passage directly from Fanon's work which specifically refers to this subject. Writing in 1960 of the anti-colonial rebellion in the cities of the Third World, he says:

> The rebellion, which began in the country districts, will filter into the towns through that fraction of the peasant population which is blocked on the outer fringe of the urban centers, that fraction which has not yet succeeded in finding a bone to gnaw in the colonial system. The men whom the growing population of the country districts and colonial expropriation have brought to desert their family holdings circle tirelessly around the different towns, hoping that one day or another they will be allowed inside. It is within this mass of humanity, this people of the shanty towns, at the core of the *lumpenproletariat*, that the rebellion will find its urban spearhead.

For the *lumpen-proletariat,* that horde of starving men, up-
rooted from their tribe and from their clan, constitutes one of
the most spontaneous and the most radically revolutionary
forces of a colonized people.[23]

However, the strategy of PCV and MIR did not produce
the results for which it had been designed. In fact, as their
extremist campaign got under way, their influence and prestige among the barrio people began to decline noticeably,
reaching a low point at the end of 1963, as was so clearly
reflected by the public response to the December elections.
Three factors had a direct bearing on the extreme leftist parties' loss of support.

1. The calculation of the barrios "ripeness" for revolt was
grossly inaccurate. It reflected a serious misreading of the
people's attitudes and grievances. One assumption on which
the campaign was apparently based was that many, or most,
rancho dwellers were no longer willing to tolerate the physical and economic conditions under which they lived and
hence were prepared to fight for rapid change. However, such
a view represented the essentially middle-class perspective of
the leaders of the revolutionary parties who projected their
own impression of wretchedness and misery into the minds of
the barrio people. It did not recognize that the criteria by
which barrio dwellers judged their own welfare and advancement were very different from those associated with the modern urban way of life,* nor that various aspects of barrio life
were very well suited to the needs of barrio people. (These
will be discussed in the following chapter.)

---

* John C. Turner, in his paper "Uncontrolled Urban Settlements: Problems and Policies" [184], emphasizes the opportunities for rational urban
development that have been missed because government officials have
assessed the problem of shantytowns solely in terms of the values and priorities of the affluent minority. He says that "the value of a given environment
cannot be judged from its physical appearance or material conditions. Its
value—to the lives of those that use it—can be truly determined only by the
ways in which it supports their present situation and in which it provides
them with opportunities for changing it." (1.2.2./2.) It is especially relevant
to our study to note that, in a later section (6.1.2), Turner points out that
both the "traditionally production-oriented economists" and the "orthodox
political revolutionaries," for much the same reason, have generally failed to
recognize this fact.

Another false assumption was that antagonism toward the AD-dominated regime was acute enough to induce large numbers of persons to take up arms against it. There is no doubt that there were many grievances regarding AD's role, but while they caused resentment toward the party, they did not prove the whole political mechanism a failure. According to the existing system, a voter antagonized by the party in power could back any of several alternative parties, all of which were severe critics of the government—a fact that helped discourage a sense of frustration and desperation. Besides, the parties of the legitimate opposition made abundant pledges of their commitment to improve barrio conditions. The message of the extreme left, at least as it came through to the public, was almost totally "anti," concerned solely with eliminating the evils of the AD (and, to a lesser degree, COPEI) government; it gave little assurance to the average man that he would be better off later under leftist direction.[24]

Moreover, the theoretical justification of the extremist campaign—that Betancourt and his supporters were (together with the Venezuelan "oligarchy") "puppets" of the North American "imperialists"—was not convincing to barrio men, regardless of their antagonisms toward the government. Betancourt himself had a reputation of being a nationalist and anti-imperialist (although his concept of what constituted anti-imperialist policies was far less radical than that of the extremists). He had appointed an astute and intensely patriotic Minister of Petroleum whom the barrio people could trust to keep the country's interest foremost in mind in future negotiations with the oil companies. The trade unions, dominated after 1961 by Acción Democrática, were likewise not being pushed around by the foreign firms; instead, collective bargaining had proved a lucrative procedure for members.

The persuasiveness of the extremists' argument was further weakened by the issue of "imperialism" itself having lost much of its former sense of urgency. Earlier it had not been difficult for party leaders to convince the more politically

sensitive of the barrio people that the "imperialists" were the
cause of many of their problems because the vast majority
could recognize only one visible function of the oil industry
—at that time the most conspicuous evidence of foreign (and
hence "imperialist") investment *—it provided the revenue
that enabled the Pérez Jiménez dictatorship to thrive. Virtually none of the barrio dwellers had jobs with the industry
(whose employees as a rule lived in company housing). With
the exception of barrio dwellers in Maracaibo, Cabimas and
Puerto La Cruz, the few who were able to benefit directly
from the commercial activities stimulated by the oil boom
lived in the small oil towns and did not influence attitudes
of people in the principal urban centers. The old image began to change when the Betancourt government's "no-conces-
sion" policy became effective, obliging the oil companies to
stop the rapid expansion of their operations. Subsequently
large numbers of foreigners left the country, the myriad peripheral services and firms disappeared, and the oil companies quietly moved out of the public eye.

A new understanding of the role of foreign investment
was promoted as the result of Betancourt's successful industrialization program. The new companies, located in a dozen
cities throughout the country, provided not only jobs for
barrio residents, but also a great variety of new commodities.
Most of the firms produced consumer goods—automobiles,
tires, medicine, toothpaste, deviled ham, etc.—fully appreciated by the urban public, including the poor rancho owners.
In short, it looked as if Betancourt and his party had been
able to get the "imperialists" to do some work for Venezuela,
instead of vice versa.

2. The FALN's urban guerrilla warfare proved to be a
grave tactical error. Its success in creating a climate of uneasiness and, to a lesser extent, generating a feeling of hostility
toward the government's methods of repression was more
than offset by the mood of revulsion that developed in the

---

* The two iron-mining companies, another potential object of anti-
"imperialist" accusations, did not attract much public attention since their
operations were small, in comparison to those of the oil industry, and restricted to a fairly remote area of the country.

barrios. Terrorist activities struck much too close to home for barrio families to look on dispassionately at the fate of the victims. Almost all the murdered policemen were barrio residents. In many instances, they were shot to death while walking home from work or sitting in their ranchos at night; families, friends and neighbors were witnesses. Some of those killed were elderly men who had been working for the force for years before AD came into power and were considered about as politically harmful as traffic cops. When the FALN ambushed a train just outside Caracas in September 1963, and machine-gunned to death four national guardsmen—all the sons of poor families—the disgust was especially strong because, for a barrio youth, it was a sign of social advancement to launch a career with the national guard.

Much of what the people did not learn of the horror of the terrorist campaign from personal experience they learned from government propaganda. All during 1962 and 1963 special publications printed in newspaper form were distributed throughout the barrios—full-page pictures of men lying on the pavement, half their faces blown off by machine-gun fire; bleeding children and anguished mothers; lists of the number of dead and wounded in recent terrorist attacks. Posters literally covered downtown walls with a now-famous photograph of a priest holding a soldier mortally wounded during the revolt at Puerto Cabello.[25] Radio broadcasts continually denounced the latest work of the *asesinos communistas*.

There is evidence that the urban campaign not only repelled many of those who witnessed it, but also discouraged some of those who waged it. Régis Debray, the French journalist who is very sympathetic to the Venezuelan "National Liberation" movement and who followed it closely during the peak months, suggests in a detailed analysis of revolutionary tacts in Latin America [26] that the principal factor causing the terrorists' shift from an urban to rural emphasis in Venezuela was the steady demoralization of the urban combatants. He cites the natural disadvantages of waging guerrilla war in the barrios in terms of mobility, escape routes and informers. He also attributed the guerrillas' shift away from the cities to other problems: that the combatants had no fixed base from which to work, that they had a hard time converting the barrio residents because they could do so little for them, and that they suffered from the lack of discipline and dedication that comes from not being totally involved, day and night, in the struggle, as were the rural combatants.

3. The combined government and AD offensive played a decisive role in weakening the influence of the extreme left in the barrios. The Communists and miristas were fired by the Ministry of Education, squeezed out of other government posts, and generally removed from positions of power. Many of the key organizers of the guerrilla warfare, including three congressmen, were arrested and jailed as the anti-government campaign gathered momentum, deprived of sources of assistance from the higher echelons of their parties, barrio leaders of the extreme left were severely handicapped.

After the extremists' grip on organized community leadership was broken, the new juntas dominated by AD were set up. Since these were officially delegated to sponsor desarrollo comunal, they denied the Communists an opportunity to rally support as organizers of self-help projects. The AD initiative forced them into a difficult position. It confronted the Communists with the dilemma resulting from the fact that, on the one hand, they claimed to support wholeheartedly the efforts of the barrio people to improve their conditions, and, on the other, they were vehemently and categorically opposed to government policy. What should the Communists have done, therefore, when neighbors were about to experiment with self-improvement through desarrollo comunal—join in and try to take over the leadership, or sabotage the project? Surprisingly, they seldom chose the former alternative. The reasons were probably a combination of general party tactics and the realization that AD leaders were on guard against such a move. Instead, they opted for the latter, and by doing so acknowledged their capitulation insofar as they shifted from positive to defensive action. But even defensive tactics were sometimes effective. For instance, by taking the stand that desarrollo comunal was an official trick to dupe the poor people into doing what should have been done by the government, they were able to discourage groups who otherwise might have cooperated. The very newness of officially-sponsored self-help projects looked suspicious to the barrio man who did not already have an allegiance to the governing party. Even when the program was well known, it was perfectly apparent that the projects were not supported by a politically disinterested government. And no man wanted to be "taken." To combat the effectiveness of this tactic, government agencies frequently compromised their ideals by outright provision of community improvements which were originally designed to be exercises in self-help.

More aggressive sabotage intended to damage already completed projects had varying effects. In cases where the community's participation had been slight, damage done to schools or water facilities diminished the people's appreciation of these projects and thus robbed the authorities of some of the credit due to them; in an extraordinarily short space of time, anger which was initially provoked by the extremists' tactics was transformed into irritation with the authorities who failed to make the necessary repairs. However, in barrios where a large number of families had cooperated on particular projects and had carried them through to completion, such violent attacks proved disastrous to extremists' prestige. For instance, in a Caracas barrio that hangs precariously on the edge of a cliff, a group of parents had resolved to construct a fence along the sections where there was danger of their children falling off. The task of acquiring the materials, mobilizing the neighbors, and finally building the fence was tiring and frustrating, but within about three months it was nearly completed. Then late one evening several teenagers walking along the entire course of the fence bent and twisted each of the metal posts, rendering them impossible to repair. That the boys were under the direction of the ex-junta president—a Communist—was no secret; the contention between his supporters and those surrounding the new junta president had been a central issue in the barrio for some months already. But the Communist leader had vastly underestimated the strength of the people's conviction that they themselves—and not the community-development worker who had provided the stimulus, nor the officials who had offered some materials—had been responsible for their accomplishment, of which they were proud. As a consequence, he found himself practically isolated within his own community, able to influence significantly only four or five of his closest friends.

Post-1963 Developments

The preceding discussion has been concerned primarily with the role of the political parties in barrio affairs during the period preceding the 1963 election. Largely as a consequence of the outcome of the election and what it revealed about the relative popular support for the various organizations, certain significant changes have subsequently taken place in the tactics and activities of several of the principal parties.

The extreme left's role, first of all, has undergone substantial transformation. As was noted earlier, the principal component of the extremists, the Communist party, has publicly abandoned its sponsorship of violent opposition to the national government and, thereby, has dissociated itself from (and in turn has been disowned by) the still militantly revolutionary Fuerzas Armadas de Liberación Nacional (FALN). This has meant that although the party continues to lack legal status, its present role in barrio politics, simply as a vehement critic of official policies, is now roughly equivalent to that played by the legal leftist opposition represented by PRIN. The FALN for its part has come to identify closely with the guerrilla strategy of the late Che Guevara and, more recently, Régis Debray,[27] and has shifted most of its attention from the urban centers to the "armed struggle" in the countryside. This has resulted, of course, in a considerable lessening of political tensions in the barrios.

Another important development has been the emergence of FND, the party which formed around Arturo Uslar Pietri, as a formidable force in barrio politics. Spurred on by the strong electoral support that Uslar rallied in the major cities in 1963,[28] the party moved quickly to build up its organizational strength in barrios throughout the country. Recently it has been especially active in cities where it has been able to count on the backing of its members in government offices, as in Caracas, and has organized new juntas and attempted to mobilize community action projects. It is highly probable that during the first year following the election FND was the single most popular party among barrio residents. However, the early image of Uslar as an "independent," which had been one of the strongest elements in his appeal to the urban poor, gradually lost its luster as FND had to compromise itself and its vehement anti-adeco position while participating in the coalition. FND, in power, began to take on characteristics that made it look more and more like one of the traditional parties. This was undoubtedly one of the main considerations that prompted its leaders to abandon the government in 1966 and to join the opposition. It remains for the 1968 elections to demonstrate to what extent the party has been able to maintain its favorable image among barrio dwellers and how strong a force it will become in barrio politics.

Finally, Acción Democrática has modified its behavior on the local level in that it has become less defensive and less exclusive than it was during its first administration. The party is no longer so concerned about maintaining its tight control over all group activities. While it still actively sponsors desarrollo comunal, its local officials are more willing now to accept and to encourage the participation of non-adecos and to respond positively to petitions that come in from independents. One of the interesting manifestations of the new AD outlook has been its public invitation extended to old members who defected with either the MIR (1960) or AD-OP (1962) factions to return to the fold without fear of reprisals. An obvious factor influencing AD's change has been the disappearance of a major threat from the extreme left. It is also very likely that the party leadership is concerned about the poor performance at the 1963 election as represented by the sharp decrease in the party's share of total votes and, more critically perhaps, by its inability to attract the votes of nonmembers. But, as in the case of FND, one will have to wait for the results of the 1968 elections to discover how effective AD has actually been in improving its image.*

* As final corrections are being entered on the proofs for this book (December 1968), the results of the 1968 elections are just becoming known; however, it is too soon to draw any conclusions from the incomplete data which are now available.

III

**Barrios
and
Venezuelan
National
Politics**

8

Barrios as a Force for Political Change

An accurate assessment of the significance of the barrios in national politics to date is hindered by the difficulty of identifying precisely what constitutes barrio influence. Thus far, any political influence possessed or achieved by the barrios has not been exerted directly. Seldom have they been their own spokesmen, and it is hard to determine whether the political parties who profess to play this role actually do speak for the barrios, or whether in fact they speak for their own parties but in the name of the barrios. None of the parties has "barrio wings." There are no lobbyists who pressure for barrio interests. In short, it is virtually impossible to isolate for analysis specific political decisions and reactions resulting from barrio influence. It is nevertheless clear that the barrios' very existence has had a highly significant impact on Venezuelan politics when we consider how the focus of political power has shifted during the last thirty years.

From the Wars of Independence in the early nineteenth century until approximately 1940, control of national politics was firmly in the hands of what has been called a "dinarchy" composed of the military and the agrarian élite.[1] The frequent struggles for power that characterized this period were essentially the quarrels of competing factions or families within this ruling group; they never altered the fundamental political structure. With the death of the dictator Gómez in

1935 and especially with the initiation of General Medina's administration in 1941, a relaxation in government control led to the first open expression of special political and economic interests by new social groups which had emerged as a result of Venezuela's economic transformation following the discovery and exploitation of petroleum in the early 1920's. Anxious to overcome their relative political isolation the middle sectors, as these have subsequently been termed, welcomed the initiation of a few leaders in organizing them and bringing their influence to bear on national affairs. As a consequence, a third force—the political parties—emerged to compete with the traditional powers.[2]

From 1945 to 1948 there was an interlude when the military, led by a group of junior officers, temporarily departed from its traditional conservative position and backed the newly formed political parties to an extent which enabled the parties to dominate national politics. But the tenuousness of the arrangement and the inherent weakness of the parties was made poignantly clear when in 1948 the military, increasingly unsure of its ambitious allies, reasserted its former position of authority, removed the Acción Democrática regime, and restored political power to the country's conservative interests. At that time the parties were unable to put up effective resistance.

The dominance of the conservative forces persisted until the Revolution of January 1958, when the balance of power shifted abruptly. As in 1945, dissident military elements again supported the parties; but this time an important element was introduced that had been absent before—the collective action of the Venezuelan populace. For the first time, the parties showed they could mobilize on a large scale their vast support among the lower class. Earlier this had not been possible because the Venezuelan poor, for the most part, had formerly lived scattered throughout the countryside, seldom concentrated in settlements larger than tiny *caserios*. Distances were great, and communication and transportation facilities rudimentary. Then, mainly during the years of the Pérez Jiménez dictatorship, about half a million campesinos had migrated to the cities.* No longer on the wings of the political stage, a large proportion of the nation's poor was now massed in its center. Receiving directives by radio or leaflets, the new city dwellers could congregate in vast numbers at strategic points within a few hours. Their communities could be easily seen by all the relatively affluent members of urban society; and nowhere was their existence more conspicuous than in the capital itself, where their ranchos were perched on the hillsides looking down upon the modern city.

Apparently national political leaders were slow to recognize the significance of the rural-to-urban transition, for it was not until 1957 that they moved to organize the new urban residents. Domingo Alberto Rangel, the ex-leader of MIR, has criticized both AD and the Communist party for this failure, charging they helped prolong the dictatorship by not mobilizing the "floating masses" earlier. Rangel blames the Communists in particular for having stubbornly continued to concentrate solely on the "classical proletariat," the industrial working class.[3] When the leaders finally did take the initiative they did so not in the name of their respective parties (AD, URD, COPEI, and PCV), but in that of the Junta Patriótica, a clandestine organization that was organizing and coordinating the anti-Pérez Jiménez forces. By January 1958, however, they had complete control of the political life of the barrio dwellers, and when they called on the people to rise up against the dictatorship, following the revolt of the Air Force on January 1, the response was immediate and sustained. Thousands of persons came out of their ranchos and superbloques and joined in the struggle, burning buses and officials' cars and fighting the police with sticks, rocks, and Molotov cocktails. In a long illustrated article appearing on the front page of its January 23, 1959 issue, *El Universal,* one of Venezuela's more conservative newspapers, paid special tribute to the role in the Revolution of the Caracas barrios—where "the tyranny of Pérez Jiménez met its most decided resistance." Another eyewitness account, in the book *Testimonio de la Revolución en Venezuela,* says of the

* For basis of estimate of migration see note 9, p. 183.

violence of January 21–23: "The whole band of workers' quarters in Caracas, from east to west, is ablaze with [revolutionary] fire." [4] While the violence was most concentrated in the capital, there were similar uprisings in most of the cities of the interior where the barrio dwellers were also the principal participants.[5]

For a year or so after the Revolution the parties frequently demonstrated how quickly and effectively they could mobilize the urban poor for mass action.* On July 23, 1958, when General Castro León threatened to overthrow the Provisional Government, the four major parties responded by gathering immense crowds in the central plazas of many major cities (in Caracas, for example, an estimated 80,000; 50,000 in Barquismeto; 30,000 in Cumaná) [6] as an ominous warning to the military of the vast opposition that could be expected against a military attempt to cancel out the revolutionary gains. Again, in the early morning of September 7, 1958, when the authorities discovered another plan for a coup, the political leaders succeeded by mid-day in staging similar mass demonstrations in Caracas and elsewhere.[7] To celebrate the first anniversary of the Revolution and to honor the visit of the recently triumphant Fidel Castro, party leaders repeated the performance in January of 1959. *El Universal* reported that they succeeded in congregating 100,000 persons in the Plaza El Silencio. This was the last occasion on which the various parties cooperated in rallying their backers; the euphoria of the immediate post-Revolution era wore thin and the bitter election campaign eroded the sentiment for united action. However, while the parties have subsequently tended to act independently of each other, such demonstrations have remained effective. AD getting its supporters

---

* The term "the political parties" as used in this section refers collectively to all the major parties—including those formed after 1958. Although in the present context we are discussing the role this "political group" (the two other major groups being the military and the business elite) plays in the national political system, the reader should recall the limits of an *individual* party's ability to mobilize the barrios described at the end of Chapter 5— namely, that, with the exception of opposition parties in Caracas, only those parties that share government power on the municipal or state levels are really effective.

to cheer their approval at inaugurations of public works in Maracaibo, or FDP organizing its backers for a mass march on the capitol building in Caracas, or the Communists and miristas bringing scores of rancho dwellers out on the streets of Puerto Cabello to give battle to the Army, are examples of the accumulated evidence that the barrios are enormous sources of political strength readily available to the parties.

Before examining the response of the military and the business elite—the two other groups besides the middle class party leaders that are most influential in the Venezuelan polity—to the newly acquired political asset of the parties, it is important to discuss briefly the question of the trade unions' involvement in these demonstrations, since one could erroneously assume that union members rather than barrio dwellers have been the principal participants. Often implicit in books and articles about politics in Latin American cities is the belief that organized labor is the only segment of the urban lower class capable of collective action, and that it is therefore the only group meriting much attention. This view is reflected in the frequent tendency to devote whole chapters or sections to the development and role of the labor unions, but only two or three sentences to the sprouting in recent years of "vast slums" of the unemployed and underemployed. A more explicit statement of this general attitude is found in James L. Payne's book, *Labor and Politics in Peru,* where, in his introductory remarks, the author dismisses the possibility of Lima's "barrio" (called *barriada* in Peru) dwellers playing an active role in national politics, saying "For the political scientist they (the barriadas) are, contrary to popular belief, of little importance because the highly disorganized state of the migrants precludes sustained, concerted political activity." [8] In the Venezuelan case, however, we know it has been the barrios, not the trade unions, which have been the dominant element in the various demonstrations mentioned above; while union leaders, mainly in their capacity as party leaders, have assisted in organizing a number of these political activities, the rank and file members have not played a major role. We know, for example, from the statements of Fabricio Ojeda, the head of the Junta Patriótica, that at the time of the Revolution its leaders had not yet succeeded in infiltrating organized labor sufficiently to count on its cooperation. In a speech on January 24, 1958,[9] Ojeda explained that his organization had ordered the burning of buses and automobiles to tie up transportation because it did not have control of the transport union. Newspaper reports, personal observation, and conversations with persons who have participated in the demonstrations, indicate that most of those involved have come from the barrios and, in Caracas, from the superbloques—areas where union members are quite few. Furthermore, many of the post-January 1959 demonstrations have been organized by political parties or leaders that have no appreciable influence on organized labor. For example, in January 1963 the founders of FDP, the party which supported the candidacy of Larrazábal, managed to get many thousands of persons down to the Caracas airport to greet that popular hero when he returned to Venezuela after an absence of four years.[10] Similarly, URD gathered some 10,000 of its supporters in front of the state assembly in Maracay in mid-1963 to protest an alleged unfair maneuver by Acción Democrática. Finally, even party leaders who enjoy control over segments of the labor movement would clearly prefer to use barrio dwellers for their mass activities because they are a much cheaper political resource. Lacking cohesion and internal discipline, they are in a weak position to demand compensation for their "public services." The unions, on the other hand, with a well-organized labor federation and with representation in the government through the Ministry of Labor, are much better able to compel political leaders to reward their support.

Appreciation of the new-found power of the political parties has undoubtedly been one of the most effective restraints on military intervention in the civilian government of Venezuela since 1959. John J. Johnson anticipated this situation when he wrote of Latin America in general a few years ago: "As the masses become ever more politicized and learn more about how to make revolutions, the cost in lives of suppressing popular uprisings can be expected to rise to a level where the armed forces will be reluctant to extract it, either in the interest of civilian groups or on their own behalf." [11] Intervention by the military could not only be severely taxing on the nation's resources; it could also be self-defeating. Edwin Lieuwen, emphasizing Betancourt's influence on the attitudes of military officers, says "he warned them that their whole institutions might be annihilated by an aroused populace, as had happened in Cuba, should they attempt to reimpose a dictatorship of the Pérez Jiménez type." As a consequence, "most top officers now appear to understand that military rule is probably the surest way to provoke the outright destruction of their entire organization by a thoroughly vindictive, anti-military civilian populace." [12] The officers' unwillingness to step in uninvited on numerous occasions when the fabric of Venezuela's political life seemed to be severely threatened indicates they may indeed have concluded that their interests in long-term stability can be best safeguarded by their support of a moderate and well-organized, popularly-based party.*

Recognition of the parties' ability to exploit collective action by the urban poor has also certainly been a strong factor in persuading the business elite to accept and support the new political system. This group, composed principally of industrialists and oil company executives, but also including bankers and owners of commercial firms, has emerged only in the last forty years as a product of the enormous expansion of the Venezuelan economy. As its strength grew it rapidly began to pre-empt the dominant position among the economic elites which had been maintained for generations by the traditional agrarian-based families.[13] Yet while its economic be-

---

* To be sure, there have been various other factors which have influenced the military's decision not to intervene. Important among these have been Betancourt's conciliatory policy toward the Armed Forces (see Alexander, *The Venezuelan Democratic Revolution, op. cit.*, pp. 105–117) , the relatively calm and confident attitude of the business community (see Frank Bonilla, "The National Perspectives of Venezuelan Elites," in Bonilla and Silva, eds., [50], p. 32) , and the firm public support given to the AD administration by both the civilian and military branches of the United States Government. But while these factors served to discourage intervention, especially during the Betancourt period, they did not alter the basic power relationship between the military and the parties which is of course the decisive deterrent.

havior has been highly progressive by Venezuelan standards, its political ideology has been identified with a system of government allowing for very limited popular participation. Even today the model administration for many businessmen remains that of General Isaías Medina Angarita (1941–45) which was overthrown by the Acción Democrática-led coup. However, since the Revolution, the business elite has developed a genuine respect for the power of political parties and this has greatly increased its willingness to accept a political system which the latter dominate.[14] The most convincing evidence of the new attitude of Venezuelan big business has been its much-expanded public role in both political and social spheres.

In the political area businessmen have formed their own organizations as pressure groups to deal with and influence the political parties and the government. One such organization, Asociación Pro-Venezuela, was founded in 1958 to represent primarily the interests of the middle-level industrialists and businessmen. John Friedmann, in his study of the evolution of the involvement of the business community in the national planning process, compares its role in the Venezuelan polity to that of the Americans for Democratic Action (ADA) in the United States.[15] Another organization which received more international attention because it was sponsored by a number of Veneuzela's most prestigious industrialists was Acción Venezolana Independiente (AVI). Formed in late 1962, AVI's original function was to provide financial support to the campaigns of the various political parties in exchange for influence over the selection of candidates, as assurance that the business community's interest would be taken into account by the next government.[16]

In the social field the business elite's activity has been no less notable. Many of its members believe that the group's by now customary contributions to the alleviation of the nation's social problems—in the form of capital investment, production of consumer goods and creation of new sources of employment—are no longer sufficient to meet the growing demands of the poor. This conviction has been expressed in their sponsorship of a variety of private programs—Fé y Alegría, YMCA, ACCION en Venezuela, and Instituto Venezolano de Acción Comunitaria—designed to attack the country's social problems. Perhaps the most dramatic expression of the business elite's concern was the Maracay Conference of Executives in February 1963, attended by virtually all leading industrialists, bankers, and heads of commerce, who actively participated in four days' intense discussion of how they might pool their resources—both money and talent —to help the Venezuelan poor improve their lot rapidly enough to ensure the peaceful and evolutionary development of the nation. Out of the conference emerged an imaginative and ambitious plan, Dividendo de la Comunidad, which called on all private firms to contribute annually a certain percentage of their profits to a community fund that would be channeled into the various existing social programs.[17]

In order to understand more clearly the transformation of the Venezuelan power structure it is useful to see it in the conceptual framework provided by Charles Anderson in his thesis about the Latin American political system.[18] Anderson introduces two terms to help explain how political power is won and consolidated by competing groups in the development of national politics. One is "power contender" for an individual or a group which seeks to have its demands implemented by government machinery. The other is "power capability," defined as "a property of a group or individual that enables it to be politically influential." As Anderson puts it, "Possession of a power capability is the price of admission to the political arena." [19] Adapting the Anderson concept to the Venezuelan situation, we note that from approximately 1940, when they began organizing openly, until 1958, the middle-class party leaders were power contenders without convincing power capabilities. As a consequence, their principal rivals, the military and the economic elites, were able to maintain ultimate control over the course of national politics and to sanction or prohibit political party functioning without the necessity of serious regard for repercussions. However, this situation changed with the Revolution when the parties' leaders demonstrated their possession of a new power capability, their capacity to mobilize mass action by the urban poor. At this time the leaders gained full access to the political arena and were able to set the style and rules of the new system.* Although they are still subject to certain definite limitations—the traditional power contenders, after all, remain in the arena—the political party leaders now manage the conduct of national politics.

The special significance of the fact that so many of the lower class persons whose political life the parties control are city dwellers is underlined by Anderson's reference to "the urban bias of the Latin American political systems." [20] He emphasizes that, to be successful, power contenders must be able to "demonstrate possession of a power capability sufficient to pose a threat to existing contenders." If a particular political resource is too distant from the groups it is meant to impress, it will not be perceived as a threat. This is why, Anderson explains, a student strike may be effective in provoking a response from the government while a full-scale agrarian revolt may not.**

---

* While it is probably obvious, it is important to mention specifically that the role in the Venezuelan polity that has been ascribed here to the barrios is quite different from that James L. Payne ([136]) has ascribed to organized labor in Peru. There, he says, labor has used the threat of violence to pressure for governmental response to specific demands, such as a wage increase. Although he calls this pattern of political bargaining a kind of "democracy by violence," he does not mean by this that "democratic" parties or governments have used labor either as a bulwark against military intervention or as a tool to overthrow "non-democratic" regimes.

** Anderson apparently overlooked this crucial point about the geographic location of the power capability in another article, " 'Reformongering' and the Uses of Political Power," ([97]) in which he discusses the survival of the Acción Democrática administrations. He implies that by "tapping the virtually unexploited reservoirs of discontent that lay outside the major cities" (p. 33), AD has used the campesinos to threaten the other power contenders in the same way that we are maintaining the barrios have been used. Although he is not explicit he possibly has in mind that on various occasions AD has brought large numbers of campesinos into the cities to demonstrate on the party's behalf—for instance, during the riots in Caracas in October–November, 1960 (*The New York Times,* November 1, 1960), and the uprisings in Carúpano and Puerto Cabello in 1962, and for the first anniversary of Betancourt's inauguration (*The New York Times,* February 14, 1960). However, the validity of Anderson's implication is subject to doubt. First, on each occasion the AD campesinos were clearly used to impress the opposition parties and to offset strong leftist support among the

Unaggressive Political Behavior

It is clear that the barrio dwellers' considerable influence on Venezuelan national politics thus far has resulted not nearly so much from their own actions as from their potential for action. Except during January 1958 the barrio people have not actively asserted themselves on their own behalf, nor have they forced changes in current development. At the same time, despite constant prompting by leaders of the extreme left, their political behavior has been notably nonviolent and unaggressive.

To many outside observers, this would seem paradoxical. Barbara Ward's remarks about the political problems created by rapid urbanization in the developing nations reflect the anxiety felt by many who have seen the barrios and have assumed that their residents have all the essential ingredients of a truly revolutionary force.

All over the world, often long in advance of effective industrialization, the unskilled poor are streaming away from subsistence agriculture to exchange the squalor of rural poverty for the even deeper miseries of the shanty-towns, favelas and *bidonvilles* that, year by year, grow inexorably on the fringes of the developing cities. They . . . are the core of local despair and disaffection—filling the *Jeunesse* movements of the Congo, swelling the urban mobs of Rio, voting Communist in the ghastly alleys of Calcutta, everywhere undermining that all too frail structure of public order and thus retarding the economic development that alone can help their plight. Unchecked, disregarded, left to grow and fester, there is here enough explosive material to produce in the world at large the pattern of a bitter class conflict finding to an increasing degree a racial bias, erupting in guerrilla warfare, and threatening, ultimately, the security even of the comfortable West.[21]

---

urban poor. They were not meant to discourage impending coup attempts. Second, if the military were planning to intervene it is improbable that AD's capacity to mobilize the campesinos would be an effective deterrent, since the military could quickly and easily deprive the party of this source of support merely by blocking the two or three main highways and one railroad that offer the only access to the capital city from the interior.

Another writer, speaking specifically about the Venezuelan barrios, says: "The squatters often make up such a great part of the urban population . . . and are so discontented that their mere presence threatens political and social instability." [22] Observations of the same kind are frequently found in the columns of the foreign journalists who visit Caracas and report on the political problems facing the nation.* In order to explain the wide gap between outward appearance and reality, and to understand why barrio residents have not been more politically aggressive, we need to examine more closely the effect both of their attitudes and of the political system.

SOCIAL AND POLITICAL ATTITUDES

The most obvious explanation for the lack of assertiveness is the barrio people's diffidence toward direct and unsanctioned political action, a characteristic which, if the earlier analysis is correct, is largely the consequence of their lack of confidence in themselves as political actors, distrust of their leaders, and insecurity in the ominous presence of "authority." Without these inhibitions barrio dwellers—at least those who live in the cities of the interior—might be more easily mobilized by the opposition parties and transformed into militant supporters. Moreover, with a feeling of greater security they would be more likely to produce their own leaders (of an extra-community sort) who could organize them and represent their collective interests.

However, outward appearance is most deceptive in the impression it gives about the barrio people's own attitudes toward their way of life. Despite the apparent wretchedness of rancho living, it is not a bitter experience for the great majority. It does not make them feel oppressed or victimized by the rest of society, nor does it engender an acute sense of social injustice. This is, of course, not what one would think

* William Mangin, in his survey of studies on squatter settlements in Latin America ([126], pp. 66–67 and 82), makes a special point of trying to dispel what he calls the "myth" about the revolutionary, "festering-sore" characteristics of the squatters. He quotes several amusing and even absurd remarks made by alarmed observers, Latin American as well as North American.

if one assumes that the residents evaluate their conditions by modern middle-class criteria. Nor is it the impression one gets from reading the much publicized diary of a Brazilian favela dweller in São Paulo, *Child of the Dark.* Passages such as the following characterize the mood of the book: * "Our world is the outer edge of civilization. Do you know where I sleep? Under bridges. I'm going crazy. I want to die." And elsewhere: "There is no meaning in my life . . . the day is sad as my soul . . . I think that my insipid life was too long." [23] Without attempting to analyze the personality or perspective of Carolina María de Jesus, the author, or to explain the special characteristics of the favela life that she experienced in São Paulo it will have to be enough to say that one should not, on the basis of her book, generalize about attitudes of shantytown dwellers in other areas, and certainly not in Venezuela.

From the vantage point of their residents, there are a number of aspects of the barrios that make life there not only tolerable but, in many cases, actually appealing—largely because of what might be called a unique atmosphere of personal freedom that permeates this whole sector of urban society. One reason is that barrio people's physical mobility is virtually unlimited. They can shift their residences from city to city, from barrio to barrio, unhampered by fears of official repression. They can travel about within their respective cities and not feel restricted by social pressure to any given sections. Nor do barrio residents feel confined to a job by economic exigencies. Nobody is "born into" an industry, believing himself tied to that industry irrevocably until he is too old to work any more. A great many have no employment, and so do not feel committed to stay in one place waiting indefinitely for new jobs to be created. If they do stay, they do so of their own accord, usually because they can live off relatives without worry about going hungry. Even the fully employed man, if he wearies of factory labor in Valen-

---

* That these particular passages are cited by the noted sociologist William McCord ([173], Chapter 2) to illustrate the plight of migrant peasants in the cities of the developing nations suggests how pervasive this image of shantytown living probably is.

cia, for instance, can easily resign, receive his severance pay, and set up a bodega in his rancho, or, if he is so inclined, seek his fortune in the diamond fields of Guayana.

Influenced strongly by their egalitarian outlook, barrio residents also have a high appreciation of social mobility. Since they are not inhibited by a notion of their own inferiority, they tend to believe that the road to social and economic advancement is open for them. The degree to which this belief prevails was amazingly well confirmed by the CENDES-CIS survey. When rancho dwellers were asked if any capable person could become an owner of a large enterprise or a high government official, between 86 and 90 per cent answered in the affirmative. Such an attitude, of course, does a great deal to discourage frustration and to relax class consciousness. Or, as S. M. Lipset has indicated, where there is a *belief* in the prospects of social mobility, there is a "corresponding reduction in collective efforts at social change." [24]

The aura of commotion and excitement that characterizes urban, as opposed to rural, life, heightens the sense of freedom resulting from mobility. Barrio men do not feel hemmed in by boredom. Honking horns, street vendors hawking their wares, newspaper boys dashing through the streets, political party propaganda, neon advertisements, blaring radios, pretty girls in bright dresses—all these constantly remind them that the city is full of activity to satisfy their desire for diversion. Similarly, they have daily contact with a variety of persons of different occupations, political allegiances and even, occasionally, social classes. All this points up the fact that they do not share the experience of "isolation" which according to Lipset contributes heavily to the political extremism of miners, sailors, lumbermen, sheep-shearers, and others elsewhere in the world. [25]

What probably enhances the sense of personal freedom in barrio living more than any other single factor is the luxury of having "property." A rancho is a man's private house, and it rests on land he considers his own. He can convert it into a dance hall and paint it orange and black to attract customers.

With sufficient savings he can construct a sturdy cinder-block home and, if space permits, add rooms as his family grows. Or, if he needs cash, he can sell all this and move on. The spirit created by this freedom for improvement and expansion (or "lack of controls," as one U.N. consultant prefers to call it) [26] is vastly different from that which is characteristic of the slums in the industrialized cities of more developed North American and European countries, where working-class families live in buildings which belong to absentee landlords and pay high rent for shabby quarters; where physical improvements have to wait for the landlord's initiative; and where tenants are evicted at his discretion. The psychological effect of this relationship on families who are not able to enjoy the advantages of a developing economy is well known.

Something approximating this industrialized urban mentality appeared in the superbloques built during the Pérez Jiménez regime in Caracas, which were until very recently Venezuela's most authentic example of real slums. The largest group of these, "*23 de enero*," which houses between 100,000 and 125,000 persons, consists of 38 separate units, fifteen stories tall, some 200 yards long, and only one apartment wide. Seen from a distance, they look like gigantic concrete dominoes set on their sides. When the government administrative controls broke down immediately after the 1958 Revolution, barrio families crowded into the still-vacant apartments, attracted by prospects of free quarters already equipped with running water and electricity. Completely unprepared to utilize properly the semi-modern facilities of the buildings, such as toilets and garbage chutes, and unused to the confining aspects of apartment living, they soon created an atmosphere of destitution unknown in most barrios. Although many families never paid any rent and government agencies had little control over their affairs, the degrading experience of living in such inhospitable quarters was certainly one reason the parties of the extreme left were able to gain complete dominance over political life in the superbloques. During the terrorist campaign in 1962–1963, the supporters of PCV and MIR converted "23 de enero" into a fortress which the police dared approach only in a battalion armed with machine guns.*

Charles Stokes has made a distinction between what he calls slums of "hope" and slums of "despair,"[27] which serves well to contrast the prevailing mood in the barrios with that of ghetto-like areas in more industrialized countries. Rather than impede the continued social and economic advancement of new city dwellers as inner-city ghetto living does, the barrio actually facilitates such advancement by providing inhabitants with free land, a certain security of tenure, and the opportunity to invest in their own improvement.[28] Because they recognize the potential for improvement, rancho dwellers tend to be hopeful rather than despairing about their future, as their replies to the CENDES-CIS survey reveal. 69 per cent said (in 1963) that they thought that their situation would improve in the next five years and, when asked if there was anything that their families needed now that they did not expect to get in the same period of time, 56 per cent answered "No." **

A person unaware of the positive aspects of life in a barrio as seen by those who live there might easily conclude, after comparing the sanitary, housing and spatial conditions in the cities with those of the countryside, that migrants from the country to the city must have suffered a substantial setback.[29] However, while this may be the personal opinion of

* The period from 1965 to 1967 saw substantial improvement in the conditions of "23 de enero" largely because many of the "barrio-type" families who were unwilling or unable to make the payments moved out at that time rather than pay rent as demanded by the housing administration.

** Myron Weiner's analysis of election results in Calcutta ([193]) offers an interesting parallel. Contrary to what had often been assumed, he found that dissatisfaction and extremist voting was much less prevalent among the newly arrived migrants who lived in the shantytowns and were most materially deprived than among the more settled lower-class families of the central districts. Mangin ([126], p. 91, note 6) remarks of Oscar Lewis's concept of the "culture of poverty" that while it is applicable to certain lower-class housing areas, especially in the central slums, it is definitely not appropriate for the majority of squatter settlements. Speaking of the "barrio" dwellers in Latin America, Mangin says: ". . . they are not alienated, hopeless people caught in a vicious circle of poverty. For most of the adults their condition in the squatter settlements is the best of their lives and a marked improvement on their previous two or three houses."

the outside observer, it is not shared by the majority of barrio dwellers. An officially sponsored study of urban problems in Valencia by a French consulting firm found that, in the attitudes of barrio families toward migration, ". . . there is a deep note of optimism in these motivations. In-migration resents a positive picture for the poorer people. It has the aspect of a conquest." [30] Various other studies suggest that the belief that urban life, despite certain disadvantages, is better than rural life, prevails among shantytown dwellers in most of Latin America.*

Barrio attitudes toward class relations must be mentioned because if the rancho dwellers were actually budding revolutionaries it would probably be reflected in their antagonism toward the affluence of the upper strata of urban society. Although there is little empirical evidence to substantiate a claim one way or the other, two important factors point to the probability that barrio dwellers' sense of a "class struggle" is relatively weak. First, each of the political parties (including presently the Communist) promotes the view that society is an integral organism in which members of each class find it to their mutual benefit to cooperate with members of the others.** None of the political parties wants to have the image of a one-class party. FDP comes nearest to being exclusively a barrio party (in the central cities), but not from choice. COPEI and FND, both of which get most of their backing from the middle class, have worked hard to broaden their base by soliciting the support of the lower class, and FND's efforts have been particularly successful in many urban centers. Consequently, barrio dwellers have had little incentive to look inward and weld together exclusive class interests. Second, the image of the urban rich has undergone considerable change in the years since the Revolution.

* Mangin ([126], p. 89) writes that at least one source from every country surveyed stated that the urban squatters were more satisfied with their present situation than they had been in the rural areas.

** This is certainly not the impression one gets from reading the Acción Democrática manual ([42], pp. 6–8), which analyzes in considerable detail the exploiting and semi-feudal nature of *la burguesía,* composed of commercial importers, bankers and industrialists, but the party's daily conduct of government affairs clearly reveals a far more moderate outlook.

Previously, under the Pérez Jiménez dictatorship, the rich were held generally responsible for poor living conditions because at that time the most ostentatiously wealthy Venezuelans were closely associated with the government, and were known, or believed, to have amassed their enormous fortunes through official channels, at the expense of the poor. Later, however, after many of these men were run out of business or forced to leave the country, popular opinion came to identify the rich with the cement manufacturers, the owners of sugar refineries, breweries, and soap factories, and with the presidents of advertising and shipping firms, and utility companies—industrialists and businessmen who, today's barrio resident tends to believe, have earned their wealth. He sees a vague relationship between their advanced education and industriousness on the one hand, and their economic achievement on the other. He is not, therefore, so suspicious of their activities and does not assume they are harmful to his interests. On the contrary, he believes, by making new jobs available, they can provide him with a good opportunity for advancement. That barrio residents now have a generally favorable attitude toward the wealthy is evidenced by the fact that, when asked by the CENDES-CIS interviewers whether they thought big businessmen were good for the country, 59 per cent answered positively and only 15 per cent negatively.

THE POLITICAL SYSTEM

The relatively unassertive role of the barrios in national politics thus far must be attributed in part to the nature of Venezuela's political system. The present system emasculates the collective strength of the barrio people by dividing their allegiances among several antagonistic parties, thereby leaving them unable or, perhaps more precisely, unwilling to unite and speak with a single voice on the big issues of their barrio existence. Unemployment, for example, is the single most prevalent grievance; but when one of the parties tries to rally the discontented around it—as, for instance, the *Larrazabalistas* did in Caracas toward the end of the Betancourt administration—the protest is all but drowned in the fury of partisan competition. Furthermore,

there is always at least one party—the government party—
that would prefer to avoid such issues altogether, lest they
draw too much attention to the party's own inadequacies.
Looking back at January, 1958 we find that the absence of
party rivalries (the parties then being bound together in the
Junta Patriótica) was one of the principal reasons the barrio
dwellers participated so actively in the Revolution.

Additionally, leaders of the parties which control political
activities in the barrios almost all see themselves as having an
important stake in the present political system, whether this
be the salary their organizations pay them, the respect and
prestige gained from holding public office, the excitement
and sense of self-importance got from participating in the
debates on the floor of the Congress, or the prospect of shar-
ing in the benefits of political power on the local level. Even
the opposition party leaders are generally not interested in
jeopardizing the existence of the present system by fomenting
violence that might lead to military intervention: the leaders
of PCV and MIR, two parties which were obviously unwilling to play by the rules of the game during the Betancourt
administration, have subsequently concluded that their best
interests lie in working with, not against, the system. To appreciate the importance of this situation it is useful to contrast it with that which has developed in the last few years
among the urban Negro population in the United States,
another politically marginal group but one which, as was
noted earlier, lacks much of the hopefulness evident in Venezuelan barrios. In the big U.S. city ghettos the most dynamic
political organizations, which are steadily attracting greater
allegiance from politically sensitive Negroes, are those associated with the concept of "black power" which openly rejects
some of the principal tenets of the contemporary U.S. political system, claiming that it serves only the interests of the
white majority. While these groups may not have played a
leading role in the riots that have erupted in Los Angeles,
Newark, Detroit and elsewhere, there can be little doubt that
they, and the growing popularity of the political sentiments
they represent, have encouraged the tendency to look outside

the system for means of pressing demands, and hence to resort to violence.

The Venezuelan system also deters the barrios' assertiveness by giving to one party—the party of the President—great powers to regulate the political affairs of the urban poor. As we have seen in the discussion of Acción Democrática, the President can channel his authority down through his various ministries, governors' offices, prefectos, and junta federations and thus severely but legitimately hamper the opposition parties' ability to consolidate support and further disrupt stability. Of course, if such power were carried too far, it could easily cause resentment and hatred among the populace. However, the Venezuelan government has been extremely sensitive to this possibility and has managed, especially under Betancourt's direction, to maintain a delicate balance between permissiveness on the one hand and control on the other.[31] In this way it has avoided creating an acute sense of repression among the barrio populace.

These inhibiting features of the political system must be appreciated to understand the relatively unassertive role of the barrios since 1958, but another factor is of fundamental importance—that barrio dwellers, in the years since the Revolution, have been able to take their first steps toward integration into the national political system. Because of the importance of this factor, which entails a variety of problems related to the future political role of the barrio sector, it will be examined separately in the next and final chapter.

9

Political Integration

As the term is used here, political integration refers to the ability of a group or sector of society to ensure that the demands it makes on the political system are responded to positively by the political decision-makers. This ability depends largely on the group's possession of an Andersonian power capability sufficiently threatening to the power-holders that they feel obliged to take the group into account. But it can also depend on the existence of what might be called "bonds of sympathy" based on ideological, class, or personal considerations which provide special lines of communication between the group, or its leaders, and the holders of power. This second factor is highly significant in Latin America where the practice of politics is still relatively uninstitutionalized and the emphasis on personal ties extremely strong. It has played an obvious role, for instance, in securing the privileged status of the landed aristocracy in the area's traditional military dictatorships. It has also contributed significantly to the effectiveness of the urban middle and upper classes in the Venezuelan polity.

Before considering the particular case of the barrios it will be helpful in clarifying this concept of political integration if we briefly examine two sectors at opposite ends of the political integration spectrum. The most obvious example of extreme political isolation would be the campesinos under the Pérez Jiménez dictatorship. They possessed virtually none of the assets which might have enabled them to ensure governmental response to their needs. In particular, they lacked the capacity to strike (which a rural proletariat would have), the opportunity to translate their vast numbers into votes, and the ability to threaten the urban-based power-holders with collective violence. At the other extreme, the Venezuelan business community, as it operates in the present political system, exemplifies a group which is highly integrated politically. Among its political assets enabling it to rely on a responsive government are control of important economic resources; ability to provide significant financial support to the political parties and thus exert direct influence; its own political and economic organizations; and its class identity with most of the top government officials as well as its members' personal acquaintance with important political decision-makers.*

Under the Pérez Jiménez regime, barrio residents were almost as politically isolated as the campesinos. Although they benefited more than the campesinos from the effects of rapid economic growth, they were able to get practically no direct response from the government to their demands. During this period, settlement of new barrios was tightly controlled, and even when new settlers managed to secure plots for ranchos, they found that the government provided no communal facilities. Employment opportunities through municipal and state agencies were extremely limited, and most of the few such available jobs were in Caracas, to which the dictator allocated about 50 per cent of total government spending.[1] As the economy developed, jobs were created in the private sector, especially with the construction industry, but steady migration and immigration meant that only a

---

* In reality the sectors are not so consistently integrated as this brief description suggests. For example, one of the middle-level businessmen's advantages over big business is their ideological identification with certain principles of government policy, particularly in regard to national planning. As another writer in the field has explained ([57], p. 45), this identification has enabled middle-level businessmen to work out an arrangement with the government for direct participation in the formulation of national plans. The more conservative big businessmen, who resisted government intervention in the private sector, have forfeited this opportunity for influence.

minority of the barrio population were ever lucky enough to benefit. Social amenities such as school and medical facilities were virtually ignored.

Opportunity for political expression was frustrated even more severely. Although twice, during the ten-year period between the overthrow of the Gallegos government in 1948 and the fall of Pérez Jiménez, Venezuelans were asked to go to the polls, at neither time were they given a meaningful choice. The first time, in 1952, their decision was annulled when the dictator discovered they had not supported him; the second time, in late 1957, they were told to answer merely "yes" or "no" to whether they wanted Pérez Jiménez to continue in power. Legal activities of the political parties were restricted almost to the point of extinction; party leaders who were not jailed, murdered, or exiled had to operate underground. Freedom of expression and of assembly was effectively throttled by the ubiquitous secret police.

In view of the barrio dwellers' inability to secure governmental response to their material and political demands it was not surprising that they joined enthusiastically with the students and dissatisfied military officers when the party leaders sought their help in revolting against the Pérez Jiménez regime and replacing it with a system which reputedly was well designed to attend to barrio needs.

The post-1958 political system has fulfilled some of the barrio dwellers' expectations insofar as it has assured them that the present holders of power are sensitive to their two main political assets—their large voting strength as a group, and their ability to act collectively under the leadership of one or more of the political parties. Under the new system Venezuelan government officials, on all levels, feel compelled to concern themselves with the barrios' basic social and economic requirements because they recognize that, if they were to ignore these, they would risk being removed from office— either by an election, if the barrio vote should be captured by an opposition party, or by a coup, if the military should decide no longer to tolerate the political instability stemming from barrio discontent.

The present system also gives barrio residents of relative political sophistication an opportunity to realize some of their political aspirations. Since they have the option of joining any party, they can satisfy their desires to belong, to serve a useful political function, to associate with men of influence, and, if they choose to be members of a dominant party, to identify themselves with the government. The existence of such a variety of parties seeking lower-class support means that for almost everyone politically inclined there is an organization to which he can appeal to champion on a higher level his particular cause. Only the relatively few who look to the illegal parties of the extreme left for leadership and representation are excluded from this privilege at present. Additionally, the system allows even those without party affiliation the freedom to voice their complaints, speak out in protest against official policy, and solicit assistance with no fear of reprisal.

In spite of scant published evidence, there is reason to believe that by Latin American standards the Venezuelan political system has been relatively successful—if measured by political effectiveness and attitudes—in dealing with the problem of political integration of the urban lower class. Among Latin American nations of the greatest political development, it appears that Venezuela compares favorably with Chile [2] and Mexico,[3] although it is apparently a good way behind Puerto Rico, where Tumin and Feldman say there is an "extraordinary, widespread feeling of genuine control of affairs on all levels." [4]

However, while the political status of barrio dwellers has improved substantially since the Revolution, and this has contributed to their relatively unassertive role in the Venezuelan polity, it is nonetheless obvious that the degree of political integration which they enjoy is very limited, for although they are no longer ignored by the political decision-makers, they have little or no real effective control over the decisions that are made. Actions by government officials affecting the barrio sector—for example, the initiation of a housing project, the formation of a junta federation, or the promotion of an industrial development program—are taken without any participation by the barrios or their representatives, and consequently whatever benefits the barrios obtain are determined entirely by the government's officials and the latter's own assessment of barrio needs in relation to political expediency and national economic priorities. Indicative of this non-participatory role is the fact that the only official specifically representing the barrios in government circles is the junta federation president, who not only functions on a very low official level (and consequently is handicapped by a scarcity of funds), but is also the appointed political agent of the government party. This feature of the barrios' political status contrasts sharply with that of the trade union members who are solidly represented at the highest level of national government by the Ministry of Labor, and by the quasi-governmental Confederación de Trabajadores de Venezuela. Similarly, although the middle class does not enjoy such formal representation, it has adequate substitutes in the "bonds of sympathy" that link its members closely with the political decision-makers, and in its own organizations such as the Federación de Cámaras de Comercio y Producción, Acción Venezolana Independiente, Asociación Pro-Venezuela, and Rotary and Lions Clubs, which can exert effective pressure nationally and locally.

Within the Anderson context this situation suggests that the barrios' power capabilities are only partially developed, and that most important political decision-makers therefore do not feel seriously pressured by their use. The effectiveness of their voting strength, in the first place, is weakened by several factors. Venezuelan voters go to the polls only once each five years, and the results of this one election determine the entire network of officials who have authority to influence the barrio dwellers' lives: governor, state officials, prefecto, junta federation president, municipal council members, and other municipal officials. The absence of interim elections of course means that voters have little opportunity to express disapproval (or approval) of the officials' performance that might bring about better results. Since state officials, **junta**

federation president, and prefecto are all appointed by the
state governor (who himself is appointed by the national
President) , and since party slates of municipal council members are determined at a level high above barrio influence, all
these officials tend to consider themselves more accountable
to their own parties, and to their government superiors, then
to their barrio constituents. The sense of security against the
effect of a possibly adverse barrio vote which this characteristic fosters among the government officials is reinforced by the
fact that the election is above all else a national affair, and
hence tends to focus the public's attention more on national
issues and party leaders, than on the performance of municipal and state governments. Theoretically, the barrios' ability
to elect their own juntas could partially compensate for the
limited effectiveness of their vote at the national election,
since juntas might offer an interim opportunity to present
their case to the higher authorities; but in fact the juntas are
rarely adequate for this purpose. Having no official status,
juntas have no real power vis-à-vis the authorities, a fact that
is made all too clear by the informal procedure for submit-
ting their petitions and the arbitrariness with which these are
dealt by government officials. If an official is uninterested in
listening to their complaints or requests, he has no legal or
constitutional obligation to do so. An even greater disadvantage of the juntas is that they seldom represent the people of
the communities, but rather the interests of a municipal or
state government.

Similarly, the effectiveness of the barrios' second main
power capability, their potential for collective action, is
weakened by aspects of the present political system which
were discussed in the previous chapter. The ability of barrio
dwellers to formulate and then express a collective will is
severely limited by the existence of mutually antagonistic political parties which splinter the barrio sector among various
different allegiances, and by the great power that the system
gives to the President of the Republic to control disruptive
activities of the opposition parties. To be sure, there are numerous examples of mass demonstrations organized by one or

more of the political parties, and while, in the aggregate, these have a significant effect on the political attitudes of the military and the business elite, individually they do not appear to have much influence on the municipal and state governments against which they are directed. It is possible such demonstrations might have more success in this respect were they to use violent, rather than the customary peaceful, tactics, for under such circumstances the government might feel greater need to respond, appreciating the danger of a military coup if political instability became too great. However, as we also noted earlier, virtually all opposition party leaders are unwilling to accept this alternative since they, like the government officials, have a strong interest in maintaining the current political system.

At the same time that we recognize that the political system limits the political integration of the barrios as a whole, it is important to emphasize that it favors heavily one small portion of that sector—the minority of barrio persons affiliated with the government party who can count on substantially greater attentiveness from the authorities. The political strength of this minority stems of course from the fact that the government depends heavily on its faithful support—to help make government programs operative in the barrios, maintain political stability, or simply win elections—and hence is willing to compensate it for services rendered. This dependent relationship was well illustrated by the 1963 elections, when virtually the only votes received by the dominant government party, Acción Democrática, were cast by its own members.

The proportionate size of the minority can grow, of course, as the result of a coalition arrangement which allows persons affiliated with the coalition parties to identify with the "in" group and therefore to share, in spirit if not in fact, the benefits of government attention. As more persons are brought under the coalition's umbrella, the ranks of the malcontents are weakened and partisan contention eases off. This helps explain why the political climate in the Caracas barrios became so much less bellicose under Leoni's administration than it was during Betancourt's presidency, when AD and its coalition partner, COPEI, had the support of only a small fraction of the barrio residents. Although AD's following has remained substantially the same under both Leoni and Betancourt, its new partners, URD and (until recently) FND, have solid barrio backing. But even when a viable arrangement is sustained among coalition party leaders in the Cabinet and Congress, it often does not carry down to the local level; persons who theoretically should be included in the new coalition "in" group can feel just as "out" as if they were still in the opposition. And at best the coalition arrangement offers a very tenuous solution to the problem of political integration. Such political alignments are agreed upon only when the parties involved consider the arrangement to their advantage, and if the relative strength of the partners alters during the five-year period between elections, party leaders may no longer consider it in their interests to continue to participate. This was undoubtedly one of the reasons for COPEI's refusal to join up again with AD after the 1963 elections.

Political Implications for the Future

Some of the implications of the obstacles to the continued political integration for the barrio dwellers' future role in the Venezuelan polity can be appreciated when we consider the changes in attitudes and behavior that are likely to come with the growth of the aspiring class and the coming of age of today's barrio youth. However, before examining these it must be clearly established that the "problem" of the barrios, however it is defined or interpreted, is likely to persist for a number of years, if only because the barrios themselves will persist. They are not a transitional phase of urban life that will pass away as quickly as they appeared. In fact, there is reason to believe that their size and population will increase in the near future—probably at a faster rate than other sectors of urban society.

Migration of campesinos will continue steadily, for there is no indication that the urban centers have lost any of their appeal.* On the contrary, because of such factors as the ambitious regional industrial development programs in Puerto La Cruz, Maracay, Valencia, and Puerto Cabello, the well publicized opportunities for employment in Ciudad Guayana, the construction of the bridge across Lake Maracaibo and the gradual recovery of that area's economy, and the tapering off of the terrorist campaign in Caracas, campesinos will undoubtedly continue to be attracted by the prospects of urban living and to make their trek toward the cities. Moreover, it is possible that government efforts to improve living conditions in the countryside—at least to the extent of expanding educational facilities and promoting community development—will prove, quite unintentionally, a further stimulus to young campesinos to leave home. In a study of urbanization and migration in India, it has been found that "migrants to the large metropolis possess a considerably *higher* average level of educational attainment than the general population of the states from which they are drawn," and the authors of the study conclude that if that pattern is nationwide, "it may be expected that as school attendance in the villages increases, there will be an increased flow into the cities of literate rural youth seeking their fortunes." [5] Thus too, Lucian Pye remarks on the stimulus provided by community development techniques for awakening ambitious, intelligent villagers in the developing nations to the probability that life in the cities is more rewarding. [6] Barring any drastic change by the government in urban settlement policies, the migrant campesinos can be expected to follow the usual pattern of moving in with relatives in the barrios, and periodically forming new communities.

An increase in total barrio population ** and in the num-

* The official projection for the urban population (over 2,500) for 1970 is 70 per cent of the total population; for 1975, it is 74 per cent; for 1981, 77 per cent. (See [89].) For prospects of the urban housing problem up to 1971, see [17].

** While migration is certainly the most important cause of the more rapid growth of the barrio sector, there is evidence that the natural increase may also contribute. Mangin, in "Latin American Squatter Settlements" ([126], p. 72), states that birth rates were found to be higher than national averages in all areas surveyed.

ber of barrio communities is likely to be offset only slightly by countervailing tendencies. There will be a slow but nevertheless perceptible disappearance of some old barrios as they become physically incorporated into the main body of the city or transformed into middle-class residential areas. As dirt streets are paved, and bus and por puesto transportation is provided, the value of the land rises quickly, and the original settlers begin to sell out for high profits. The communities take on a more permanent appearance: mud, cardboard, and aluminum ranchos are converted into cinder-block houses with tile roofs; sidewalks are constructed and street lighting installed; and small-scale commercial activities emerge. The final stage of the transformation comes with the appearance of two-story buildings, movie theaters, drugstores and the like. At this point, the area ceases to be referred to as a "barrio" and becomes just another city neighborhood. Evidence of this process can be seen in some barrios situated on the immediate fringes of established sections of the cities, or on choice land in city outskirts. As Lisa Peattie writes: "When you look at any Caracas barrio which has been long established (and in the Caracas context long means on the order of twenty years), the process is manifest through a stratigraphy which, as in archaeology, expresses evolutionary change through time by sequence and levels and forms. At the bottom of the hill, the dwellings are plastered and painted masonry; just above come rough block walls; at the top are the board and tin shacks. To climb the hill is to run a development history backwards." [7]

Several cities, most notably Caracas,[8] have long-term urban renewal plans for removing the most objectionable barrio blights. However, government officials are exceedingly reluctant to tackle the problem on a large scale. Some are understandably worried about political repercussions, knowing that when it has been necessary to remove whole communities—for instance, to make way for highway construction in Caracas—the ensuing furor has lasted for months. The angered rancho owners in such cases were not only adamant about holding onto their "property"; they were also completely uninterested in moving into new housing projects, far removed from the cities' centers, for which they would have had to pay rent.[9] Other government leaders have moral or ideological scruples against tampering with the barrios, as evidenced, for example, in an official 1959 report on the housing problem of Caracas which maintains that to remove the poor people from the hills would be "an inhuman act that would contravene the principles of social justice established by the democratic government of Venezuela." [10]

If Venezuela's current economic expansion keeps up, some men and women of today's aspiring class will eventually move out of the barrios, be absorbed into the middle class, and set up residence in the longer-established sections of town. Nevertheless, although no figures are available on this process, one can assume that it does not—and will not—affect many of even the aspiring class, since families generally have demonstrated a preference for remodeling their homes in the barrios rather than moving to rented quarters or buying land in some other area.

Therefore, since we can assume that barrio dwellers will for some time constitute a large part of the urban population, it is important to consider forces within the barrio sector that indicate the barrio people as a whole will become increasingly sensitive to their political status, and increasingly unwilling to tolerate it.

As the cities industrialize and traditional institutions give way under the pressure of modernization, the influence of the aspiring class increases markedly relative to that of the general class—a trend already well advanced in Caracas and Ciudad Guayana, and easily discernible at present in Valencia, where the rapid growth of a large industrial sector is being accompanied by a noticeable enlargement of the role played by aspiring-class leaders. There is every reason to think the same transformation will occur in other cities. In Maracaibo, for instance, when the economic recuperation which is already under way begins to accelerate and the introduction of new industries makes the barrio man less dependent on municipal and state agencies for employment, one can expect to see general-class control of barrio affairs energetically challenged by the aspiring class.

The waning of general-class influence on the one hand, and the growth of aspiring-class influence on the other, will have important political consequences. The general class, heavily dependent on the government for material benefits, has appreciated the importance of the vote, and freedom of party action, mainly as necessary tools for insuring that the government would look after its economic and social improvement. But the aspiring-class members, their living conditions relatively advanced, have looked upon the vote and freedom of party action more in political than in social or economic terms, as a means to assimilation into urban political life and of access to the political power-holders. Therefore it is they who will be the more greatly distressed to realize that the present political system frustrates rather than facilitates their political integration. The 1963 election has already demonstrated that it is precisely in the areas where aspiring-class influence is most concentrated that dissatisfaction with the traditional parties' management of politics is strongest. A recent analysis of the election notes that in the region referred to as the Metropolitan Center—comprising the two states of Miranda and Aragua plus the Federal District and in which the great majority of the population are urban residents living in the three semi-industrial cities of metropolitan Caracas, Maracay, and La Guiara—57 per cent of the presidential vote went to the "nonparty" (as opposed to the "traditional party") candidates, Uslar Pietri and Larrazábal, while nationally these men received only 28 per cent of the vote.[11] These results, combined with our knowledge that the two "mavericks," Uslar Pietri and Larrazábal, were far and away the most popular candidates in the barrios of the Metropolitan Center [12] are a fairly convincing confirmation of the trend we are describing.

These observations suggest that industrialization, although perhaps the only means of alleviating the enormous problems of urban poverty, may also, by hastening modernization, create a political awareness in the barrios that the Venezuelan political system, as it now functions, cannot easily accommodate. Myron Weiner, in *The Politics of Scarcity*, foresees similar problems in India and offers a word of caution in the concluding chapter that could also apply to Venezuela: "It must be recognized that economic growth, including not only increased productivity but also growth in education and mass communications, generally results in an increase in voluntary political organization, which in turn causes a widening of the gap between aspirations—or, at least, organized aspirations—and reality." [13]

The thesis that economic development often tends to promote political instability is, of course, not universally accepted. Many scholars argue that as the economic status of the urban lower class improves as the result of full-time employment, workers become ever more reluctant to support radical social change. Clark Kerr and his colleagues, having noted in *Industrialization and Industrial Man* that "worker protest in the course of industrialization tends to peak relatively early and to decline in intensity thereafter," and that "forms of overt protest become more disciplined and less spontaneous as formal organizations of workers emerge," maintain that this "secular decline in protest" is mainly owing to the greater positive attractions of industrialization: "Potential benefits to the individual worker everywhere appear to transcend the negative consequences of industrialization . . . rewards to industrial workers in earlier stages are often substantially greater than for other producer groups; the industrial workers are often a preferred group." [14] Irving Horowitz, trying to account for the reforming, as opposed to revolutionary, aspects of urban society in Latin America, explains that the middle classes have "at their disposal the urban working classes who feel they have a vested interest in the going social system." [15]

However, despite first impressions, these two sets of theories are not in basic disagreement but rather deal with two different types of protest. On the one hand are those protests derived from grievances essentially economic and social in nature—concerned with severe inequalities of wealth, low wages, and poor living conditions. On the other hand are protests derived from grievances essentially political—mainly concerned with the use of, and access to, political power. Although the two often go hand in hand, they do not necessarily have to be linked, as the situation in Venezuela demonstrates.

In 1958 the country experienced a political revolution that transferred government power from the hands of the military and their conservative allies into the hands of the popularly based political parties. Subsequently, as a consequence of energetic government action, the country began to undergo an extensive economic and social transformation which directly benefited the lower classes. These changes have enabled many barrio dwellers, and in particular the members of the aspiring class, to get steady jobs, build better homes, educate their children, and generally to become not unfavorably inclined toward the "going social system." But this relatively satisfied attitude of the aspiring classes toward their social status has not automatically made them content with their political status. Many of them still feel dissatisfaction with the handling of official power, with the advantages possessed by members of the governing party, and with their own inability to influence government policy—even though they have recently been able to enjoy a number of the benefits of a developing economy. It appears, then, that the growth of the aspiring class resulting from the expansion of industrialization and concomitant modernization will probably cause a decrease in antagonism of a social and economic nature among barrio dwellers, but that it could at the same time easily cause an increase in antagonism of a political nature.

The barrio dwellers' dissatisfaction, in the absence of substantial changes in their political status, seems even more likely to become acute as today's youth comes of age. Venezuela has one of the youngest populations of any nation in the world. According to the 1961 census, 45 per cent of all Venezuelans were then younger than fifteen, 55 per cent younger than twenty, 63 per cent younger than 25 and only

19 per cent older than 39. Or, more dramatically, in 1961 there were roughly as many children under five as there were adults past forty.[16] Of the future political role of the youngest of these, there is, of course, little that can yet be predicted with certainty. There is, however, some indication of the political behavior of the group between the ages of fourteen and twenty-three, and we can learn something of the role of the next generation from the males in that age group.

Several factors work against these youths adapting easily to their barrio status. They have grown up, for the most part, in the cities and are not aware of how much less satisfactory life in the countryside can be. Their education is more advanced than their elders'. And they have had far more exposure to the world of party politics than their parents had at the same age: a significant number have already had experience in political action, and the parties providing this experience usually are not the traditional parties. As these barrio youths grow older and are obliged for the first time to face the hard realities of barrio life, their situation will seem worse to them than it did to their parents; they will be more aware than the preceding generation of what they want and what they do not have. Although they should also be more qualified for employment, they will still find jobs very difficult to secure. (The Instituto Nacional de Cooperación Educativa (INCE) estimated in 1964 that each year 100,000 young persons place themselves on the labor market, but that the economy can absorb only 40,600 annually.) [17] At the same time, their formal schooling and their lifelong exposure to urban politics will have left them more alert to their political strength and the means available for voicing their demands.* Although some of today's barrio youths will probably be at-

---

* In regard to the impact of education on political behavior, Gabriel Almond and Sidney Verba ([159], pp. 380–381) say that their findings, which reflect a cross-national uniformity, indicate that the more educated person is more aware of the impact of government on the individual, is more likely to report that he follows politics and pays attention to election campaigns, has more political information, is more likely to engage in political discussion, is more likely to consider himself capable of influencing the government, and is more likely to be an active member of some organization.

tracted to the traditional parties by the prospects of getting
jobs and enjoying some of the benefits of power, it is likely
that the dominant trend will be in the opposite direction—
toward newly formed political organizations, such as FND
and FDP, which offer the prospect of managing local and
national politics in a way more consistent with the barrios'
interest in political integration. Therefore, although it may
find in these new parties a vehicle for better voicing its demands, the next barrio generation is likely to be more frustrated than the present one by its inability to influence the
government and force a positive response.

Conclusion

While Venezuela's present political system is apparently
well suited to satisfy the desire for political integration of the
urban middle and upper classes, as well as of the trade union
movement, in that it gives them the use of both formal and
informal channels to see to it that their interests will be taken
well into account by the political decision-makers, it does not
function in such a way as to ensure further progress toward
political integration for the barrio dwellers. Moreover, there
is substantial indication that the barrio people's sensitivity to
their political ineffectiveness and vulnerability to manipula-
tion will sharpen with time and weaken attitudes which have
thus far served to inhibit aggressive behavior.

The intensity of future barrio reaction, and the particular
form it takes, will depend on several variables about which
little that is conclusive can be said at this time. It will depend, for one thing, on the flexibility of the presently dominant political parties, in particular Acción Democrática, and
their capacity to adjust to the growing demands and assertiveness of the barrio sector. The parties will need to be willing to allow for modifications in the present system so that
the barrios can develop greater bargaining power within the
political arena. The barrios' future reaction will also depend
on the leaders of the non-traditional parties—to which the
barrio people seem to be giving greater allegiance—and on

their private ambitions, their political ideologies, and, perhaps most relevant, their ability to continue to see a stake for themselves in the present system and an opportunity to share in the benefits of power, at least on the local and state levels. Finally, the barrio dwellers' political behavior will partially depend on the growth rate of the economy, which in turn will be affected most decisively by the rate of expansion of the private industrial sector and by the state of the world market for Venezuelan petroleum. But while a substantial slowdown of industrial development would certainly serve to aggravate political dissatisfaction in the barrios, it does not follow that the steady maintenance of a high growth rate would by itself prevent the problem of political integration from becoming acute. On the contrary, continued economic growth may intensify barrio sensitivity to the problem.

In his paper on the political implications of rapid urbanization in the developing nations Lucian Pye gives us a hint of what could happen if the barrio dwellers as a group were to conclude they were making no substantial political headway. He cautions: "If instead of participation there is alienation, then an explosive situation can quickly build up which can only be constrained by the most severe forms of control." [18] In Venezuela the barrios' frustration might easily manifest itself in a tendency to ignore the conventional rules of the political system and resort to their not yet fully exploited but potentially most powerful political asset, the capacity to unite large numbers of persons in violent insurrectional action. In that event they could certainly count on political leaders of the extreme left to direct their energies and provide inspiration and training for urban guerrilla warfare.

If the Venezuelan barrios were to seek a new political system to satisfy better their desire for political integration, two Latin American models might seem especially suitable to them: that which operated in Argentina between 1946 and 1955 under the leadership of Juan Perón, and the current system in Cuba under Fidel Castro. While the composition and the style of these systems differ widely so that one risks gross over-simplication by linking them together, the two nevertheless resemble each other in ways directly relevant to the problems of integration in Venezuela, and the solutions that might be sought by barrio dwellers. Most obviously relevant is the fact that both systems give immediate attention to the welfare needs of the urban (and, in Cuba, the rural) poor; whether they do so at the expense of agricultural productivity, foreign exchange reserves, and transportation and communication systems (as in Argentina under Perón), or at the expense of the middle and upper classes and foreign investors (as in Cuba), they channel enough national resources into that sector to convince the lower class that the government is its benefactor. Just as significant, nonetheless, is the fact that both systems are able to instill in the lower classes, especially in those with a developing political consciousness, a sense of importance, privilege, and even mission that is hardly possible in a pluralistic, non-autocratic society, as exists for example in Venezuela today. By appealing directly to the urban (and rural) poor, and taking sides in the "class struggle," such systems enable this sector to identify closely with the government. The national leader becomes himself the symbol of lower-class aspirations; his party is said to be the people's party, through which—the poor are encouraged to believe—they themselves are ruling the country. Furthermore, by directing attention toward common class interests and common enemies, like "imperialism," political systems such as those of Perón and Castro add a new dimension to the usually petty political life of the poor —one that would be especially appealing to Venezuelan barrio youth, for the reasons described earlier in this chapter.

The political advantages of such systems as seen by the urban lower class are excellently described by Gino Germani in his analysis of Perónism in Argentina. Germani emphasizes the inadequacy of the most common explanation of Perón's control over the working classes—that it resulted from his demagoguery, and that the people gave up their freedom for the material benefits he offered them:

"The dictator used demagoguery, that is true. But the most effective part of that demagoguery was not the material advantages, but rather the fact that it gave the people the experience (real or unreal) that they had attained certain rights, and that they were exercising them. The workers who supported the dictatorship, far from feeling that they had been stripped of their freedom, were really convinced that they had won it . . . The freedom that they thought they had won was the concrete and immediate freedom of being able to assert their right against bosses and *patrones,* to elect representatives, to win suits in the labor tribunals, to feel greater masters of their own destinies. All this was felt by the worker, by the laboring class, as an affirmation of personal dignity . . . there is no doubt that the masses developed with Perónism an awareness of their own significance as a sector of great importance in national life, capable of exercising certain power . . ." [19]

It is true that political conditions in Venezuela today are very different from those that existed just before the rise of Perón and Castro, respectively, in Argentina and Cuba, where the advantages of a participant system had been completely denied to the lower class so that its political isolation was virtually total. However, in the realm of political behavior, subjective attitudes can count for more than objective facts, and if Venezuelan barrio dwellers were to decide that their country's present system failed to fulfil their needs and desires, they might well be attracted to a system resembling that of Perón or of Castro.

Reference Material

Notes

Bracketed numbers in the notes refer to publications listed in the Bibliography which begins on p. 191.

Notes to the Preface

1. For probably the most comprehensive study of urban squatter settlements in developing nations, see [158].

2. For the first published report on the CENDES-CIS project, see [50].

Notes to Chapter 1

1. For general discussions of the course of Venezuela's social and political development since the death of Juan Vicente Gómez in 1935, the following books are especially useful: [43] [45] [46] [49] [50] [52] [68] [70] [85].

2. [64], p. 482, Table S.21.

3. For a good assessment of Pérez Jiménez's economic policies, see [96].

4. [64], p. 467, Table S.6.

5. [22], p. 321.

6. [89], Cuadro 139.

7. [24], p. 421.

8. [89], Cuadros 117 and 130.

9. The estimate of the number of rural to urban migrants between 1950 and 1965 is derived by the following calculation, which recognizes that the three components of Venezuela's urban growth are the natural increase of the 1950 urban population; the immigrants and their offspring; and the migrants and their offspring.

   Begin with the total urban population growth of 3.3 million, which represents the 1965 population of 5.7 million less the 1950 population of 2.4 million. Deduct the total number of immigrants and their offspring. Venezuelan immigration statistics indicate a net immigration of 340,000 between 1950 and 1959 and virtually none thereafter through 1965. Assuming an even flow throughout the decade of the 1950's and a three per cent rate of natural increase (the annual rate at which the indigenous Venezuelan population grew between 1950 and 1965), this immigration would result in a 465,000 immigrant population by 1965. By subtracting 465,000 from 3.3 million, the figure for urban population growth exclusive of immigrants is 2.895 million.

Then deduct the increase in urban population resulting only from the natural increase of the 1950 urban population, which amounts to 1.553 million—or 48 per cent of the total Venezuelan population growth since 1950. By subtracting this figure, 1.553 million, from the above 2.895 million, we arrive at a balance of 1.282 million for urban population growth represented by migrants and their offspring.

To determine the number of migrants required to produce a migrant population of 1.232 million in 1965, increasing at the rate of three per cent per year, it is necessary to calculate on the assumption of a steady annual migration throughout the period. In this case the total volume of migrants would be 1.024 million, with an annual flow of 64,000 for each of sixteen years.

10. [80], pp. 1–2.

11. [157], p. 13, and [9].

Notes to Chapter 2

1. Probably the best single description of the physical appearance of the Caracas barrios is found in [24], pp. 422–423.

2. A number of articles have been written that stress the inappropriateness of the "slum" terminology for the shantytowns of Venezuela and elsewhere. See, for instance, [24], p. 424; [150]; [164].

3. For a discussion of the problems of disposing of human waste in shantytown colonies, see [157], p. 5.

4. [126], pp. 76–77.

5. For example, [125] in [114], p. 241; [143], p. 149; [134], p. 111.

6. [14], p. 36.

7. [63], p. 104.

8. [63], pp. 62–64.

9. See [16], p. 292 for comment on the outlook of Valencia barrio residents toward the city life outside their communities.

10. [170], p. 203.

11. [124] in [115].

12. [162] in [190].

13. [167], pp. 166–184.

14. See [61]; [44], pp. 85–86; also [56].

Notes to Chapter 3

1. [11], p. 12.

2. [185].

3. [158], p. 29.

4. [27]; also quoted in [157], p. 18.

5. For similar observations in Ciudad Guayana, see [3].

6. For further details on the origin of barrio names, see [14], pp. 14–15.

7. For a brief discussion of the cayapa as practised among campesinos, see [44], p. 84.

8. [158], p. 5.

Notes to Chapter 4

1. The discussion of the role of the middle sectors in this chapter is a fairly free adaptation to Venezuela of J. J. Johnson's well-known thesis set forth in [119].

2. See [73].

3. [36], p. 9.

4. [170], p. 171.

5. [170], p. 171.

6. See, for instance, [139], pp. 34–36; [137] in [114], pp. 200–205; [131], pp. 329–341; [152], pp. 151–155; [142] in [180], p. 353.

7. [78], p. 121.

8. For an assessment of the influence the operations of the larger of the two iron-mining companies, Orinoco Mining Company, have had on the development of Ciudad Guayana, see [3], pp. 3–7.

9. Cited in [75].

10. For a discussion of this characteristic which the Economic Commission for Latin America (ECLA) calls "permeability" and finds common to many Latin American cities, see [152].

11. [16].

12. [16], p. 289, fn. 11.

Notes to Chapter 5

1. An excellent survey of many of the studies which have noted the reluctance of villagers and peasants to cooperate for their common good is found in [166], esp. pp. 44–142. See also [181], cited in [73] in [50], p. 198.

2. This and other projects carried out by the Maiquetía barrio have been described in detail by the community leader who was the main force behind them. See [38], pp. 8–9.

3. [61], p. 68.

4. [170], p. 202.

5. [73], in 50, pp. 220–221.

6. [142] in 180, pp. 356–357.

Notes to Chapter 6

1. See [145].

2. For page references to [139] [137] [131] [152] and [142], see note 6, Chapter 4.

3. [151], in [114], pp. 122–123.

4. For the founder's own description of this project, see [74], in [92]. For an independent evaluation by a housing expert, see [2].

5. For an interesting and relevant discussion of the role revolutions play in the politicization of the masses in Latin America, see [110] in [115].

6. [10], p. 72.

7. For a description of the election campaigns of the various parties, see [72].

8. [55], pp. 3–5.

9. [31], p. 34.

10. [84].

Notes to Chapter 7

1. All percentages given in this section relevant to the 1963 elections are calculated from figures in [86].

2. [94], pp. 267–268.

3. This feature of opposition parties was suggested to the author by [183] in [186], p. 203.

4. [31], p. 31.

5. [31], p. 31.

6. [42], p. 24.

7. Unless otherwise stated, all figures on AD membership are taken from [70], p. 223, Figure 7.

8. [31], p. 34.

9. Betancourt described the decision to end the Plan de Emergencia in a televised statement made on May 20, 1963, and reprinted in [91], p. 53.

10. [33].

11. For similar observations about the connection between AD and the Movimiento by an apparently objective political commentator see [31], p. 34.

12. See, for example, [84]; and Richard Schaedel and Robert Wisdom, "Community Development in Venezuela" (mimeographed) Agency for International Development, Caracas, February 1962.

13. The three types of community development programs—"integrative," "adaptive," and "project"—which are differentiated in United Nations literature are discussed in [175], p. 12.

14. [88], p. 18, Table 1.

15. A similar attitude of another government agency faced with the problem of self-help projects in Caracas is reported in [13], pp. 3–4.

16. For explanations of the aims of COMUN, see [60] and [76].

17. For a list of the individual grants that the Movimiento and its affiliated juntas received through 1963, see [59].

18. [32], p. 22.

19. [31], p. 34.

20. A detailed list of these and other episodes is found in [85], pp. 528–531.

21. For relevant comments about the way in which the various police forces, especially in Caracas, aggravated the situation during this period, as the result mainly of their lack of experience, training, and organization, see [53], pp. 55–56, and [41] in [50], pp. 463–464, fn. 33.

22. [77], esp. pp. 80–81.

23. [165], p. 103.

24. For one of the few expressions of this "message" in English, see [65], pp. 2–23.

25. This and other photographs used by the government appear in [91].

26. [21], pp. 42–51.

27. Debray's major work is "Revolution in the Revolution?: Armed Struggle and Political Struggle in Latin America," [105].

28. [70], p. 361.

Notes to Chapter 8

1. [68], p. 157.

2. For a succinct and perceptive summary of the course of political change in Venezuela from the death of Gómez to the Revolution of 1958, see [45] in [50], pp. 39–43.

3. [77], pp. 80–84.

4. [83], p. 37.

5. *The New York Times*, January 23, 1958, pp. 1–2.

6. *El Universal,* July 24, 1958. The major role played by the barrio and superbloque dwellers of Caracas is also specifically mentioned in [77], p. 226.

7. *El Universal,* September 8, 1958; *The New York Times,* September 8 and September 9, 1958.

8. [136], p. 15.

9. *The New York Times,* January 25, 1958.

10. *El Universal,* January 13, 1963, pp. 1 and 22.

11. [118], p. 256.

12. [67], pp. 88–91.

13. For a useful discussion of the changing character of Venezuela's upper-class membership and the emergence of the business elite, see [85], pp. 91–93.

14. The new attitudes of the business elite toward the political implications of Venezuela's social problems are frequently referred to in the editorials of *El Universal,* the newspaper which most closely represents the interests of the business community. See, for example, [69], p. 4; and [54], p. 14. For remarks of various members of the business elite which illustrate support for the political system, see [51], pp. 305–306.

15. [57], p. 42.

16. For notes on AVI and other public activities of the business elite, see [47], pp. 32–34.

17. For the proceedings of the Maracay Conference, see [79].

18. First presented as a paper at Vanderbilt University in 1962, the hypothesis has subsequently been somewhat revised and published as Chapter 4 in [96].

19. [96], p. 91.

20. [96], p. 105.

21. [191], pp. 191–192, cited in [193].

22. [113], p. 542.

23. [117].

24. [172], pp. 253–254.

25. [172], pp. 87–88, 112–113, etc.

26. [188].

27. [182].

28. The part the slums of "hope" play in the steady advancement of the new and poor urban residents is most thoroughly analyzed in the writings of John C. Turner. See especially [184].

29. See, for example, the remarks of Janine Brisseau, who did a detailed study of physical conditions in the barrios of Petare in eastern Caracas, in [14], p.31.

30. [16], p. 236.

31. For a discussion of permissiveness and control with regard to the policies of the governments of the developing nations toward the new labor movements, see [163]. The lengths to which Betancourt went to preserve civil liberties in the face of constant harassment are described in [46]; see especially Chapter 9.

Notes to Chapter 9

1. [68], p. 97.

2. [112].

3. [159] and [142].

4. [147], pp. 170–171.

5. [161] in [186], p. 53.

6. [177], p. 24.

7. [35].

8. [8].

9. See, for instance, [27].

10. [11], p. 78.

11. [70], p. 359.

12. [70], p. 361.

13. [192], p. 258.

14. [170], pp. 194–197 and 208–210.

15. [116], p. 28.

16. Figures based on statistics in [89].

17. [63], p. 104.

18. [178], p. 89.

19. [108], pp. 243–249.

Bibliography

I. Venezuela

A. MATERIAL DIRECTLY RELATED TO BARRIOS AND BARRIO
DWELLERS, INCLUDING MIGRATION

[1] Abouhamad, H. Jeanette. "Estudio de El Pedregal." Caracas: Universidad Central de Venezuela, Economía y Ciencias Sociales, 1959.

[2] Abrams, Charles. "Draft of Memorandum on Housing Finance in Venezuela" (mimeographed). Submitted to the Director of the Banco Obrero. Caracas, 1960.

[3] ———. "Report on the Development of Ciudad Guayana in Venezuela" (mimeographed). Cambridge, Mass.: Harvard–M.I.T. Joint Center for Urban Studies, 1962.

[4] ACCION en Venezuela. *Year End Report, 1964.* Caracas, 1965.

[5] Banco Obrero. *Análisis del Problem de la Vivienda en Maracaibo.* Caracas: Oficina de Programación y Presupuesto, 1963.

[6] ———. *Experiencia en Desarrollo Comunal Urbano.* XI Conferencia Internacional de Servicio Social, Rio de Janeiro, 1962. Caracas, 1962.

[7] ———. *Más Viviendas para el Pueblo.* Caracas, 1963.

[8] ———. *El Problema de los Cerros en el Area Metropolitana, Informe Preliminar sobre el Cerro Piloto.* Caracas, 1954.

[9] ———. *Programación de Vivienda.* Vol. 2. Caracas: Oficina de Programación y Presupuesto, 1963.

[10] ———. *Proyecto de Evaluación de los Superbloques.* Caracas, 1959.

[11] ————. "El Rancho y El Superbloque," Anexo XII in Banco Obrero, *Proyecto de Evaluación de los Superbloques* [10].

[12] ————. *Serie sobre Estudios e Investigaciones Sociales.* Folleto No. 1. Caracas, 1962.

[13] Boyd, Osborne and Frank Servaites. "Report of the Housing and Slum Clearance Team" (mimeographed). Caracas: U.S. Agency for International Development, 1962.

[14] Brisseau, Janine. "Les 'Barrios' de Petare: faubourgs populaires d'une banlieue de Caracas," *Les Cahiers d'Outre-Mer* (Bordeaux), XVI, 61 (January–March 1963).

[15] Cannon, Mark W. and Carlos M. Morán. *The Challenge of Urban Development in Valencia.* Caracas: Foundation for Community Development and Municipal Improvement, 1966.

[16] C.I.N.A.M. *Plan de Crecimiento del Distrito Valencia.* Caracas: Editorial Arte, 1963.

[17] Comisión para el Desarrollo Urbano y la Vivienda. *Informe.* Caracas, 1964.

[18] Comité de Remodelación de Barrios. *Programa Preliminar para la Remodelación de Barrios, Area Metropolitana de Caracas (10 años).* Caracas: Oficina Municipal de Planeamiento Urbano, 1962.

[19] Consejo Interamericano Económico y Social. *Causas y Efectos del Exodo Rural en Venezuela.* Washington, D.C.: Organización de los Estados Americanos, 1954.

[20] Corrada, Rafael. "The Housing Development Program for Ciudad Guayana" (mimeographed). San Juan, Puerto Rico: University of Puerto Rico, Housing Policy Seminar, 1966.

[21] Debray, Régis. "Latin America: The Long March," *New Left Review,* XXXIII (September–October 1965).

[22] Friedmann, John. "Economic Growth and Urban Structure in Venezuela," *Cuadernos de la Sociedad Venezolana de Planificación* (Caracas, September 1963); reprinted in *Ekistics,* XVIII (May 1964).

[23] Grooscors, Rolando. "Problemas de la Vivienda Urbana en Venezuela," *Congreso Latinoamericano de Sociología.* Vol. 2. Caracas, 1961.

[24] Jones, Emrys. "Aspects of Urbanization in Venezuela," *Ekistics,* XVIII (December 1964).

[25] MacDonald, John Stuart. "Migration, Economic Conditions and Welfare in Ciudad Guayana" (mimeographed). Cambridge, Mass.: Harvard–M.I.T. Joint Center for Urban Studies, 1966.

[26] ———. "Migration and the Population of Ciudad Guayana" (mimeographed). Cambridge, Mass.: Harvard–M.I.T. Joint Center for Urban Studies, 1966. This paper is to appear as a chapter in Lloyd Rodwin, ed., *Regional Planning for Development: The Experience of the Guayana Program of Venezuela.* Cambridge, Mass.: The M.I.T. Press, 1968.

[27] Matos Mar, José. "Informe sobre las Zonas de Ranchos de Párate Bueno y Pinto Salinas" (carbon copy). Caracas, 1960.

[28] ———. "The Problem of Slums in South America," *Ekistics,* XV (May, 1963).

[29] McGarry Raymond. "Report on Water Supply and Sewage, Housing and Slum Clearance—Venezuela" (mimeographed). Caracas: U.S. Agency for International Development, 1962.

[30] Montesino Samperio, José V. "La Población del Area Metropolitana de Caracas," *Separata de Cuadernos de Información Económica.* Caracas: Corporación Venezolana de Fomento, 1956.

[31] Moro, Gabriel. "¿Por Qué Perdió A.D. en Caracas?", *Momento* (May 5, 1963).

[32] Movimiento Pro-Desarrollo de la Comunidad. *ABC de la Comunidad.* Caracas: Imprenta Municipal, 1966.

[33] ———. *Estatutos.* Caracas: Imprenta Municipal, 1963.

[34] Núñez Miñana, Horacio. "Las Migraciones en Venezuela," *Cuadernos de la Sociedad Venezolana de Planificación,* III (Caracas, May 1964).

[35] Peattie, Lisa R. "Social Issues in Housing" (mimeographed). Catherine Bauer Wurster Memorial Lectures. Cambridge, Mass., 1966.

[36] ———. "Social Mobility and Economic Development" (unpublished manuscript). 1966. This manuscript is to appear as a chapter in Lloyd Rodwin, ed., *Regional Planning for Development: The Experience of the Guayana Program of Venezuela.* Cambridge, Mass.: The M.I.T. Press, 1968.

[37] ———. "The View from the Barrio" (unpublished manuscript). Cambridge, Mass., 1965. This manuscript was published by The University of Michigan Press under the same title in 1968.

[38] Peña, Angel Ramón. "Breves Apuntes sobre Desarrollo Comunal en el Departamento Vargas" (mimeographed). Caracas: Instituto Venezolano de Acción Comunitaria, 1965.

[39] Ravell, Carola. *Anaco, Una Comunidad en Marcha.* Caracas: Oficina Central de Coordinación y Planificación, 1961.

[40] Sanabría, Tomas José. "Los ranchos—aflicción urbana," *Desarrollo Económico,* III, No. 1, 1966.

[41] Slote, Walter H. "Case Analysis of a Revolutionary," in Bonilla and Silva, eds., *Studying the Venezuelan Polity* [50].

B. VENEZUELAN POLITICS, SOCIETY, ECONOMY, AND RURAL LIFE

[42] Acción Democrática. *La Cartilla del Militante.* Caracas: Secretaría de Propaganda, 1961.

[43] Acedo Mendoza, Carlos. *Venezuela: Ruta y Destino.* Barcelona: Ediciones Ariel, 1966.

[44] Acosta Saignes, Miguel. "Algunos Aspectos Sociales del Problema de la Vivienda Rural en Venezuela," *Congreso Latinoamericano de Sociología,* Vol. 2. Caracas, 1961.

[45] Ahumada, Jorge. "Hypothesis of the Diagnosis of a Situation of Social Change: The Case of Venezuela," in Bonilla and Silva, eds., *Studying the Venezuelan Polity* [50].

[46] Alexander, Robert J. *The Venezuelan Democratic Revolution.* New Brunswick, N.J.: Rutgers University Press, 1964.

[47] "Atlantic Reports: Venezuela." *Atlantic Monthly* CCXI, May 1963.

[48] Banco Central de Venezuela. *Memoria, 1959.* Caracas, 1960.

[49] Betancourt, Rómulo. *Política y Petróleo.* México, D.F.: Fondo de Cultura Económico, 1956.

[50] Bonilla, Frank and José A. Silva Michelena, eds. *Studying the Venezuelan Polity.* Cambridge, Mass.: Center for International Studies, Massachusetts Institute of Technology; and Caracas: Centro de Estudios del Desarrollo, Universidad Central de Venezuela, 1966. A hard-cover edition of this collection has subsequently been published under the title *The Politics of Change in Venezuela: Vol. I, A Strategy for Research on Social Policy.* Cambridge, Mass.: The M.I.T. Press, 1967.

[51] Bonilla, Frank. "The National Perspectives of Venezuelan Elites," in Bonilla and Silva, [50].

[52] Brito Figueroa, Federico. *Historia Económica y Social de Venezuela.* Caracas: Universidad Central de Venezuela, 1966.

[53] Cárdenas, Rodolfo José. *La Insurrección Popular en Venezuela.* Caracas: Ediciones Catatumbo, 1961.

[54] Chávez, C. R. "La Nueva Clase Gerencial de Venezuela," *El Universal,* January 14, 1963.

[55] Commission to Study the Fiscal System of Venezuela. Carl Shoup, Director. *The Fiscal System of Venezuela.* Baltimore, Md.: The Johns Hopkins Press, 1959.

[56] Fairchild, David. "Report on El Palmar" (mimeographed). Cambridge, Mass.: Harvard–M.I.T. Joint Center for Urban Studies, 1962.

[57] Friedmann, John. *Venezuela: From Doctrine to Dialogue.* Syracuse, N.Y.: Syracuse University Press, 1965.

[58] ———. *Regional Development Policy; A Case Study*

of Venezuela. Cambridge, Mass.: The M.I.T. Press, 1966.

[59] Fundación para el Desarrollo de la Comunidad y Fomento Municipal. *Memoria y Cuenta, 1963.* Caracas: Empresa El Cojo, S.A., 1964.

[60] ————. *Objectives, Organization, Functions and Programs.* Caracas, 1962.

[61] Hill, George W., and José A. Silva Michelena, and Ruth Oliver de Hill. "La Vida Rural en Venezuela," *Revista de Sanidad y Asistencia Social,* XXIV (January–April 1959).

[62] Instituto de Estudios Políticos para América Latina. *Venezuela, Estudios de Actualidad.* No. 5. Montevideo, 1964.

[63] Instituto Nacional de Cooperación Educativa. *Publicaciones de la Presidencia, 1961–64.* Caracas, 1965.

[64] International Bank for Reconstruction and Development (IBRD). *The Economic Development of Venezuela.* Baltimore, Md.: The Johns Hopkins Press, 1961.

[65] Lairet, Germán. "The Armed Revolt in Venezuela," *Revolution* (Paris), Vol. I, No. 10, (1964).

[66] Lerner, Daniel. "Conflict and Consensus in Guayana," in Bonilla and Silva, [50].

[67] Lieuwen, Edwin. *Generals vs. Presidents.* New York: Frederick A. Praeger, 1964.

[68] ————. *Venezuela.* London: Oxford University Press, 1961.

[69] Mancera Galleti, Angel. "La Acción Empresarial," *El Universal,* January 4, 1963.

[70] Martz, John D.. *Acción Democrática: Evolution of a Modern Political Party in Venezuela.* Princeton, N.J.: Princeton University Press, 1966.

[71] ————. "The Growth and Democratization of the Venezuelan Labor Movement," *Inter-American Economic Affairs,* XVII, (Autumn 1963).

[72] ————. *The Venezuelan Elections of December 1, 1964.* Washington, D.C.: Institute for the Comparative Study of Political Systems, 1964.

[73] Mathiason, J. R. "The Venezuelan Campesino. Perspectives in Change," in Bonilla and Silva, [50].

[74] Mendoza, Eugenio. "The Housing Problem," in Wilgus, [92].

[75] Peattie, Lisa R. "Conflicting Views of the Project: Caracas vs. the Site," (unpublished manuscript). 1966. This manuscript is to appear as a chapter in Lloyd Rodwin, ed., *Regional Planning for Development: The Experience of the Guayana Program of Venezuela*. Cambridge, Mass.: The M.I.T. Press, 1968.

[76] Prieto Figueroa, Luis B. *El Desarrollo de las Comunidades* (speech in Congress). Caracas: Imprenta Municipal, 1962.

[77] Rangel, Domingo Alberto. *La Revolución de las Fantasías*. Caracas: Ediciones OFIDI, 1966.

[78] Ravard, Rafael Alfonso. "El Desarrollo de Guayana," *Política* (Caracas), 41–42 (August–September 1965).

[79] Seminario Internacional de Ejecutivos. *La Responsabilidad Empresarial en el Progreso Social de Venezuela*. Caracas, 1963.

[80] Silva Michelena, José A. "Cultural Development and Cultural Heterogeneity in Venezuela" (mimeographed). Cambridge, Mass.: Massachusetts Institute of Technology, 1966.

[81] ———. "Nationalism in Venezuela," in Bonilla and Silva, [50].

[82] Taylor, Philip B. "Democracy for Venezuela?" *Current History*, (November 1966).

[83] Umaña Bernal, José, ed. *Testimonio de la Revolución en Venezuela*. Caracas: Tipografía Vargas, S.A., 1958.

[84] United Nations. *Report of a Community Development Mission to Venezuela*. Department of Economic and Social Affairs, 1965.

[85] United States Army. *Area Handbook for Venezuela*. Washington, D.C.: U.S. Government Printing Office, 1964.

[86] Venezuela, República de. Consejo Supremo Electoral. *Resultado de las votaciones efectuadas el 10 de Diciembre de 1963.* Caracas, 1964.

[87] ———. División de Desarrollo de la Comunidad. *Desarrollo de la Comunidad en Venezuela.* VII Reunión de la Asamblea de Gobernadores de Banco Interamericano de Desarrollo, México, D.F., 1966.

[88] ———. División de Desarrollo de la Comunidad. *Report on the National Program of Community Development in Venezuela.* World Congress of Nutrition, 1963. Caracas: Central Office of Coordination and Planning, 1963.

[89] ———. Ministerio de Fomento. *Anuario Estadístico de Venezuela, 1957–1963.* Caracas: Dirección de Estadística y Censos Nacionales, 1964.

[90] ———. Oficina Central de Coordinación y Planificación. *Plan de la Nación, 1965–1968.* Caracas, 1965.

[91] ———. Secretaría General de la Presidencia. *Govierno y Nación Defienden en Venezuela el Régimen Democrático.* Caracas, 1963.

[92] Wilgus, A. Curtis, ed. *The Caribbean: Venezuelan Development.* Gainesville, Fla.: University of Florida Press, 1963.

II. *Latin America*

[93] Adams, Richard N. "The Community in Latin America: A Changing Myth," *The Centennial Review of Arts and Science,* VI (1962) .

[94] Alexander, Robert J. *Communism in Latin America.* New Brunswick, N.J.: Rutgers University Press. 1957.

[95] Amado, Jorge. "Invasion of Cat Wood," in *Shepherds in the Night.* New York: Alfred A. Knopf, 1967.

[96] Anderson, Charles W. *Politics and Economic Change in Latin America.* Princeton, N.J.: D. Van Nostrand Co., Inc., 1967.

[97] ———. " 'Reformmongering' and the Uses of Political Power," *Inter-American Economic Affairs,* XIX, No. 2 (Autumn, 1965) .

[98] Bazzanella, Waldemiro. "Industrialização e Urbanização no Brasil," *América Latina* (Rio de Janeiro), VI, No. 1 (January–March 1963).

[99] Briones, Guillermo and José Mejía Valera, *El Obrero Industrial.* Lima: Instituto de Investigaciones Sociológicas, 1964.

[100] Bonilla, Frank. "Rio's Favelas," *American Universities Field Staff: East Coast South America Series,* VIII, No. 3 (1961).

[101] ————. "The Urban Worker," in J. J. Johnson, ed., *Continuity and Change in Latin America.* Stanford, Calif.: Stanford University Press, 1964.

[102] Bossana, Luis. "Los Partidos Políticos y la Sociedad de Masas," *Congreso Latinoamericano de Sociología.* Vol. 1, Caracas, 1961.

[103] Browning, Harley L. "Recent Trends in Latin American Urbanization," *The Annals of the American Academy of Political and Social Science.* Vol. 316, 1958.

[104] Dillon Soares, Gláucio Ary. "Desarrollo Económico y Radicalismo Político" in Joseph A. Kahl, ed., *La Industrialización en América Latina.* México, D.F.: Fondo de Cultura Económica, 1965.

[105] Debray, Régis. "Revolution in the Revolution?: Armed Struggle and Political Struggle in Latin America." *Monthly Review* (special issue). Vol. 19, No. 3, July–August 1967.

[106] Dorselaer, Jaime and Alfonso Gregory. *La Urbanización en América Latina.* 2 vols. Bogotá: Centro Internacional de Investigaciones Sociales de FERES, 1962.

[107] Germani, Gino. "Inquiry into the Social Effects of Urbanization in a Working-class Sector of Greater Buenos Aires," in Hauser, [114].

[108] ————. *Política y Sociedad en una Epoca de Transición.* Buenos Aires: Editorial PAIDOS, 1962.

[109] Germani, Gino and Kalman Silvert. "Politics, Social Structure and Military Intervention in Latin Amer-

ica," *Archives Européennes de Sociologie,* II, No. 1
(1961).

[110] Goldrich. Daniel. "Toward the Comparative Study
of Politicization in Latin America," in Dwight B.
Heath and Richard N. Adams, eds., *Contemporary
Cultures and Societies of Latin America.* New York:
Random House, 1965 [115].

[111] ———. "Toward an Estimate of the Probability of
Social Revolution in Latin America," *The Centennial Review of Arts and Sciences,* VI (1961).

[112] Goldrich, Daniel, Raymond B. Pratt, and C. R. Schuller. "The Political Integration of Lower Class Urban
Settlements in Chile and Peru: A Provisional Inquiry" (mimeographed). New York; Annual Meeting of the American Political Science Association,
1966. This paper has subsequently been published as
Volume III, No. 1, of *Studies in Comparative International Development,* 1967–1968.

[113] Haar, Charles M. "Latin America's Troubled Cities,"
Foreign Affairs (April 1963).

[114] Hauser, Philip M., ed. *Urbanization in Latin America.* New York. UNESCO, 1961.

[115] Heath, Dwight B., and Richard N. Adams, eds., *Contemporary Cultures and Societies of Latin America.*
New York: Random House, 1965.

[116] Horowitz, Irving L. "Urban Politics in Latin America" (mimeographed). Conference on "The Role of
the City in the Modernization of Latin America."
Cornell University Center for Housing and Environ-
mental Studies, 1965.

[117] de Jesus, Carolina Maria. *Child of the Dark.* New
York: E. P. Dutton and Co., Inc., 1962.

[118] Johnson, John J. *The Military and Society in Latin
America.* Stanford, Calif.: Stanford University Press,
1964.

[119] ———. *Political Change in Latin America.* Stanford,
Calif.: Stanford University Press, 1958.

[120] Kahl, Joseph A. "Social Stratification and Values in

Metropoli and Provinces: Brazil and Mexico," *América Latina*, VIII, No. 1 (January–March 1965).

[121] ———. "Urbanização e Mundanças Ocupacionais no Brasil," *América Latina* V, No. 4 (October–December 1962).

[122] Lambert, Denis. "L'urbanisation accélérée de l'Amérique Latine et la formation d'un secteur tertiaire refuge," *Civilisations* (Brussels), XV, Nos. 2–4 (1965).

[123] Lewis, Oscar. "The Folk-Urban Ideal Types," in Philip M. Hauser and Leo F. Schnore, eds., *The Study of Urbanization*. New York: John Wiley and Sons, Inc., 1965.

[124] ———. "Urbanization without Breakdown: a case study," in Dwight B. Heath and Richard N. Adams, [115].

[125] Lopes, Juares Rubens Brandão. "Aspects of the Adjustment of Rural Migrants to Urban-Industrial Conditions in São Paulo, Brazil," in Hauser, [114].

[126] Mangin, William P. "Latin American Squatter Settlements: A Problem and a Solution," *Latin American Research Review*, II, No. 3 (Summer 1967).

[127] ———. "Mental Health and Migration to Cities: A Peruvian Case," in Dwight B. Heath and Richard N. Adams, eds., *Contemporary Cultures and Societies of Latin America*. New York: Random House, 1965 [115].

[128] ———. "Urbanization Case History in Peru," *Architectural Design*, XXXIII (August 1963).

[129] Matos, Mar, José. "Migration and Urbanization," in Hauser, [114].

[130] de Medina, Carlos Alberto. *A Favela e o Demogogo*. São Paulo: Martins, 1964.

[131] Medina Echavarría, José. "Part I. A Sociologist's View," in *Social Aspects of Economic Development in Latin America*, Vol. 2. New York. UNESCO, 1963.

[132] Morse, Richard M. "Latin American Cities: Aspects of Function and Structure," *Comparative Studies in Society and History*, IV, No. 4 (July 1962).

[133] ———. "Recent Research on Latin American Urbanization: A Selective Survey with Commentary," *Latin American Research Review*, I, No. 1 (Fall 1965).

[134] Nash, Manning. *Machine Age Maya—The Industrialization of a Guatemalan Community*. Glencoe, Ill.: The Free Press, 1958.

[135] Nilo Tavares, José. "Marginalismo Social, Marginalismo Político?", *Revista Brasiliera de Estudos Políticos*, XIII (January 1962).

[136] Payne, James L. *Labor and Politics in Peru*. New Haven, Conn.: Yale University Press, 1965.

[137] Pearse, Andrew. "Some Characteristics of Urbanization in the City of Rio de Janeiro," in Hauser, ed., *Urbanization in Latin America*.

[138] Rabinovitz, Francine F., Felicity M. Trueblood, and Charles J. Savio. *Latin American Political Systems in an Urban Setting: A Preliminary Bibliography*. Gainesville, Fla.: Center for Latin American Studies, 1967.

[139] Ríos, José Arthur. "El Pueblo y el Político," *Política* (Caracas), No. 6 (February 1960).

[140] Rosenblüth López, Guillermo. "Problemas Socio-Económicos de la Marginalidad y la Integración Urbana" (mimeographed). Santiago: Universidad de Chile, 1966.

[141] Rycroft, W. Stanley, and Myrtle M. Clemmer. *A Study of Urbanization in Latin America*. New York: United Presbyterian Church of the U.S.A., 1962.

[142] Scott, Robert E. "Mexico: The Established Revolution," in Lucian W. Pye and Sidney Verba, [180].

[143] Silvert, Kalman H. and Frank Bonilla. "La Educación y el Significado del Desarrollo: un Estudio Preliminar" (mimeographed). United Nations: Department of Economic and Social Affairs, 1961.

[144] Stepan, Alfred. "Political Development Theory: The Latin American Experience," *Journal of International Affairs*, XX, No. 2 (1966).

[145] Tannenbaum, Frank. "The Hacienda," in *Ten Keys to Latin America*. New York: Knopf, 1962.

[146] Tinoco Richter, César and M. T. Bruni Celli. "Los Problemas de la Mano de Obra: El Cambio Social en La América Latina," *Congreso Latinoamericano de Sociología,* Vol. 2. Caracas, 1961.

[147] Tumin, Melvin M. and Arnold S. Feldman. *Social Class and Social Change in Puerto Rico.* Princeton, N.J.; Princeton University Press, 1961.

[148] Turner, John C. "Dwelling Resources in South America," *Architectural Design,* XXXIII (August 1963).

[149] ———. "La Marginalidad urbana: ¿calamidad o solución?", *Desarrollo Económico,* III, Nos. 3-4 (1966).

[150] ———. "Lima's Barriadas and Corralones: Suburbs versus Slums," *Ekistics,* XIX (March 1965).

[151] United Nations. Economic Commission for Latin America. "Creation of Employment Opportunities in Relation to Labor Supply," in Hauser, [114].

[152] ———. *El Desarrollo Social de América Latina en la Postguerra.* Document E/CN 12/660. New York, 1963.

[153] ———. "Popular Participation and Principles of Community Development in Relation to the Acceleration of Economic and Social Development," *Economic Bulletin for Latin America,* IX, No. 2 (November 1964).

[154] ———. *La Urbanización en América Latina.* 1963.

[155] Violich, Francis, "Bibliography on Community Development Applied to Urban Areas in Latin America" (mimeographed). Berkeley, Calif.: Center for Latin American Studies, 1963.

[156] Whiteford, Andrew H. *Two Cities of Latin America.* Garden City, N.Y.: Anchor Books, 1964.

III. *General*

[157] Abrams, Charles. *Man's Struggle for Shelter in an Urbanizing World.* Cambridge, Mass.: The M.I.T. Press, 1964.

[158] ———. *Squatter Settlements: The Problem and the Opportunity.* Washington, D.C.: U.S. Department of Housing and Urban Development, 1966.

[159] Almond, Gabriel and Sidney Verba. *The Civic Culture*. Princeton, N.J.: Princeton University Press, 1963.

[160] Banfield, Edward C. *The Moral Basis of a Backward Society*. New York: The Free Press, 1958.

[161] Bogue, Donald J. and K. C. Zachariah. "Urbanization and Migration in India," in Roy Turner, ed., *India's Urban Future*. Berkeley, Calif.: University of California Press, 1962.

[162] Busia, K. A. "Social Survey of Sekondi-Takoradi," *Social Implications of Industrialization and Urbanization in Africa South of the Sahara*. New York: UNESCO, 1956.

[163] de Schweinitz, Jr., Karl. *Industrialization and Democracy*. New York: The Free Press, 1964.

[164] Emery. P. A. "Creative Aspects of Shanty Towns," *Ekistics,* XV (May 1963).

[165] Fanon, Frantz. *The Wretched of the Earth*. London: MacGibbon and Kee, 1965.

[166] Foster, George M. *Traditional Cultures: and the Impact of Technological Change*. New York: Harper, 1962.

[167] Hoselitz, Bert F. "The City, Factory and Economic Growth," *American Economic Review* (May 1955).

[168] Hoselitz, Bert F., and Myron Weiner. "Economic Development and Political Stability in India," *Dissent,* VIII (Spring 1961).

[169] Kahl, Joseph A. "Some Social Concomitants of Industrialization and Urbanization," *Human Organization,* XVIII (Summer 1959).

[170] Kerr, Clark, John T. Dunlop, Frederick H. Harbison, and Charles A. Myers. *Industrialism and Industrial Man*. Cambridge, Mass.: Harvard University Press, 1960.

[171] La Palombara, Joseph. "Italy: Fragmentation, Isolation and Alienation," in Lucian W. Pye and Sidney Verba, [180].

[172] Lipset, Seymour M. *Political Man*. London: Mercury Books, 1963.

[173] McCord, William. *The Springtime of Freedom.* New York: Oxford University Press, 1965.

[174] MacKinnon, William J. and Richard Centers. "Authoritarianism and Urban Stratification," *The American Journal of Sociology,* LXI (1956).

[175] Mezirow, Jack D. *Dynamics of Community Development.* New York: The Scarecrow Press, 1963.

[176] Mitchell, J. C. "Urbanization, Detribalization, and Stabilization in South Africa," in *Social Implications of Industrialization and Urbanization in Africa South of the Sahara.* New York: UNESCO, 1956.

[177] Pye, Lucian W. "Community Development as a Part of Political Development," *Community Development Review* (March 1958).

[178] ———. "The Political Implications of Urbanization and the Development Process," in *United Nations Conference on the Application of Science and Technology for the Benefit of Less Developed Countries, 1962, Geneva. United States Papers.* Washington, D.C.: U.S. Government Printing Office, 1963.

[179] ———. "The Social and Political Implications of Community Development," *Community Development Review* (December 1960).

[180] Pye, Lucian W. and Sidney Verba, eds. *Political Culture and Political Development.* Princeton, N.J.: Princeton University Press, 1965.

[181] Rogers, Everett M. "Motivations, Values, and Attitudes of Subsistence Farmers: Toward a Subculture of Peasantry," a paper delivered at A/D/C Seminar on Subsistence and Peasant Economies, Honolulu, March 1965.

[182] Stokes, Charles J. "A Theory of Slums," *Land Economics,* XXXVIII (August 1962).

[183] Tangri, Shanti. "Urbanization, Political Stability, and Economic Growth," in Roy Turner, ed., *India's Urban Future.* Berkeley, Calif.: University of California Press, 1962.

[184] Turner, John C. "Uncontrolled Urban Settlement: Problems and Policies" (mimeographed). United Na-

tions Interregional Seminar on Development Policies and Planning in Relation to Urbanization, University of Pittsburgh, 1966.

[185] Turner, John C. "Unpublished Lectures" (Mimeographed). 1965.

[186] Turner, Roy, ed. *India's Urban Future*. Berkeley, Calif.: University of California Press, 1962.

[187] United Nations. *Conference on the Application of Science and Technology for the Benefit of Less Developed Countries*. Washington, D.C.: U.S. Government Printing Office, 1963, p. 89.

[188] United Nations. Committee on Housing, Building and Planning. "Social Aspects of Housing and Urban Development," *Ekistics*, XXI (December 1965).

[189] United Nations. Department of Economic and Social Affairs. *Community Development in Urban Areas*. New York, 1961.

[190] United Nations Educational, Scientific, and Cultural Organization. *Social Implications of Industrialization and Urbanization in Africa South of the Sahara*. New York: 1956.

[191] Ward, Barbara. "The Uses of Prosperity," *Saturday Review* (August 29, 1964).

[192] Weiner, Myron. *The Politics of Scarcity*. Chicago, Ill.: University of Chicago Press, 1962.

[193] ———. "Urbanization and Political Extremism: An Hypothesis Tested" (Mimeographed). Cambridge, Mass., 1962.

Index